FOLLOWER

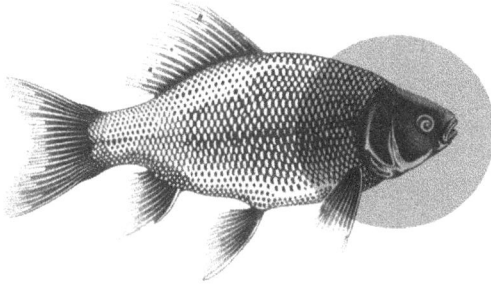

Published in the United States of America by Credo House Publishers,
a division of Credo Communications LLC, Grand Rapids, Michigan
credohousepublishers.com

Unless otherwise noted, Scripture quotations are from the Holy Bible, New
International Version®, NIV® Copyright ©1973, 1978, 1984, 2011 by Biblica,
Inc.®. Used by permission. All rights reserved worldwide.

ISBN: 978-1-62586-307-2

Cover and interior design by Frank Gutbrod
Cover photograph of author by Rose Wine Photography
Editing by Vanessa Carroll

Printed in the United States of America
First edition

Getting closer to Jesus is a lifelong journey. In *Follower*, Pastor Jennifer Layte steps into the story of Simon Peter and shares theological insight that can only be revealed by the Spirit. In her spiritually unique way, she takes us on a thought-provoking journey of Simon Peter's devoted, transformative, faith-filled, and doubtful moments. She keeps readers on the edge of their seats with great anticipation of the next turn of the fisherman's life with Jesus (and others). This book shows how God uses Simon Peter to be a model for disciples who desire to follow a closer love walk with Jesus.

—**Barbara L. Peacock**, author of *Spiritual Practices for Soul Care* and *Soul Care in African American Practice*; Founder of Peacock Soul Care

I love this book. Jennifer Layte explores the engaging journey of Simon Peter, following him from impulsive loudmouth to a rock with which Jesus built his church. If there's hope for Simon Peter, there's hope for me. Jennifer's not just a pastor and a teacher; she's a delightful writer. I barely noticed it was a study!

—**Susan Isaacs**, screenwriting professor and author of *Angry Conversations with God*

In *Follower*, Pastor Jennifer Layte takes us on an insightful journey through the disciple Simon Peter's walk of faith. Even readers who are familiar with Peter's story—or who think they are—will benefit from Layte's wisdom as she guides us through this disciple's remarkable transformation from humble fisherman to shepherd of the early church. But *Follower* is no mere biographical sketch. With warmth, humor, and a pastor's heart, Layte invites us to see our journey in Peter's and be encouraged in our own walk of faith. The path is not smooth—but it is transformational. It is, as Layte shows, the only response to Jesus holding out his hand and saying, "Follow me."

—**Lisa Deam**, author of *3000 Miles to Jesus: Pilgrimage as a Way of Life for Spiritual Seekers*

With beautifully captivating storytelling and truthful exegesis, Jennifer Layte draws the reader to put themselves in Peter's shoes and wrestle with God the way Peter wrestled with Jesus while following him. If you enjoy imaginatively engaging the lives of Jesus and his disciples, this book is for you.

—**Joash Thomas**, human rights leader, theologian, and author of *The Justice of Jesus*

When I teach from the Bible, I'm struck by how much of God's meaning we lose in our tendency to miss the *story* of the Bible. In *Follower*, Jennifer Layte invites us to see not only the facts of Jesus's good news, but the *story* of Jesus's good news inside the life of Simon Peter—and to imagine what our stories might become as followers of Jesus too.

—**Catherine McNiel**, author of *Fearing Bravely: Risking Love for Our Neighbors, Strangers, and Enemies*

FOLLOWER

How Getting Close to Jesus

Brings You to Yourself

JENNIFER A. G. LAYTE

credo
house publishers

For Dad

my first pastor

*and the man who taught me how to meet Jesus
in the pages of the Bible*

CONTENTS

FOREWORD

hristianity is a funny thing. The word *Christian* itself carries a plethora of meanings, and those connotations are largely dependent on who is doing the defining. Many of us who think of ourselves as Christians carry positive associations with the word. We are prone to policing the boundaries of the label based on adherence to certain sets of ideals. And there are those who regard Christianity and Christians with a healthy dose of skepticism, using the term to denote members of a religion regardless of their character (or lack thereof).

In the Bible, the word we now render *Christian* only appears three times (Acts 11:26, Acts 26:28, 1 Peter 4:16), and none of them in an incontrovertibly positive context. To the protest of many of my fellow Christians, I maintain that *Christian* is an amoral descriptor. When I call someone or something Christian, I am not doing it because I have noticed anything extraordinarily good *or* bad about their ethos. I use the label because they appear to have accepted (or inherited) a Christian framework for viewing and interacting with the world. They understand that Chick-fil-A is closed on Sundays because that's what God-fearing capitalists do. Saying "happy holidays" makes sense, but the impulse to lead with "Merry Christmas!" lives on. They've never thought about the likelihood that every Christina or Christopher they've ever met had at least one nominally Christian parent.

Christianity is the subtext of so much of what we understand as normal. But calling someone (or something) Christian doesn't say much about what they believe. While it can tell you a great deal about the world in which they live, if you want to learn what drives and motivates a person, you will have to observe how they move.

This is the difference between a fan and a follower. A fan may know how to blend in with a crowd, but a follower can tell you the story behind the greatest hits. A fan might own a jersey, but a follower can recount the heartbreak of a loss they didn't actually contribute to. A fan carries an affinity. A *follower carries a commitment.*

The Nazarene called Jesus had a great deal of fans. That tends to happen when you've gained a reputation for healing people for free and insisting that there is a divine blessing in store for those who find themselves estranged from civic power. The gospel accounts often refer to the fans of Jesus as "the crowds." These are the people who'd congregate en masse, hoping to catch a glimpse of Jesus and his disciples passing through town—if they weren't able to squeeze their way into the standing section of one of his sermons. Jesus shows compassion to the crowds and serves them in mighty ways. He fed thousands of them with just five loaves of bread and two fish!

The fans of Jesus showed enough enthusiasm for the world around them to take notice; however, it is the *followers* of Jesus who are called to do the heavy lifting. The followers of Jesus are called to leave their lives behind to serve the Creator of heaven and earth. And, because being a fan of Jesus is easier than being a follower of Jesus, followers fail more often than they succeed.

It is difficult to follow alone. Impossible even. Which is why Jesus calls and sends followers in groups. And Jesus commissions guides to help those who will follow in the future. One of those guides is Jennifer Layte. She's my favorite kind of guide: one who doesn't so much *lead* you as *invite* you.

I remember the first time Jenn invited me to speak at one of her retreats. She did it back before inviting someone like me anywhere was popular. It might've even been dangerous. I like to think she did it because, as wildly as our lived experiences may differ, she saw something familiar in me. You see, as outlandish as I've been known to be, I am irrepressibly curious about where Jesus is leading us. And if I had a dollar for every time that my imperfect (sometimes reckless) pursuit of the Son of God led me smack dab into Jenn's path, I'd be *much* closer to retirement.

When I learned that Jenn wrote a book about another (sometimes brash) follower of Jesus, I was convinced she'd been reading my journal. There's no other way for her to have known that I was in need of such a guide at this particular moment. In gracefully shepherding us through the story of a deeply relatable Peter, I am reminded that perfection is not a prerequisite for following Jesus. And, as engaging as this book may be, I'm grateful that she was not content to leave us readers entertained. In the pages that follow, Jennifer Layte invites us all to be *transformed*. I came to this book as a friend and fan of Jenn, and she used it to reintroduce me to another follower. I don't even think she can help it: she is forever drawn to the prospect of pilgrimage. How wonderful it is to have you along for the journey. I pray this book blesses you like it blessed me.

Trey Ferguson
Pastor of The Intention Church, theintentionchurch.com
Author of *Theologizin' Bigger*

WHY THIS BOOK AND HOW TO USE IT

I n 2019, something surprising happened. I became a pastor of a church. I guess that might not be as surprising to you as it still is to me until you know some other things about me. I am a pastor's daughter. Also a pastor's granddaughter. Also I have a brother who would make a fine pastor and even went to seminary and finished it in one shot instead of after the third attempt like I did. I guess we all probably thought he would be the one to carry on the family tradition. Besides all this, when I was growing up, even though nobody in my immediate family was overly adamant about the idea, everyone assumed that women couldn't—or at least shouldn't—be pastors, based on some passages in some of the letters in the Bible attributed to the apostle Paul. "Ministry" and "missions" were somehow okay for women in our corner of the world. Just not pastoring.

So I went into ministry/missions: overseas, working with refugees in connection with some churches in the neighborhood I was sent to. Trouble was, I was so convinced the Bible taught that women must not preach or teach when men are present that

I went far beyond the general uneasiness with the idea that I had grown up with. I turned down legitimate ministry responsibilities if men were involved because I felt like I was crossing some biblical line.

Besides, I didn't want to be a pastor or a teacher. Public speaking made me cry. In public. Teaching stressed me out. But I did love Jesus and for most of my life had wanted to introduce other people to him. And so I kept plugging away, trying to be faithful to Jesus as I knew him, and to what I believed—still believe—was his own written word (the Bible) as I knew it. Then Jesus told me to come back to the United States and didn't tell me what to do next.

Until I wrote that last sentence, I haven't been sure, for the last twenty-plus years, whether it was really Jesus who told me to come back, or whether I just made that up. But in writing this introduction to a book about a man whose own relationship with Jesus went through highs and lows, baffling interactions, and unlikely career changes, it suddenly seems a more distinct possibility that he did. Or at least that he took my in-good-faith decision and ran with it. Jesus inviting me back to a home I had never imagined returning to, Jesus not giving me any further instructions for a long time, set my relationship with both him and his book into a tailspin. But when I stopped spinning, I found that ultimately, I was on much firmer ground with both of them.

Even still, my relationship with Jesus keeps changing. He doesn't, but what I get to know about him does. As I get to know him better, my understanding of myself changes too. As my understanding of myself changes, the more I become myself. And the more I become myself, the more I see what the Bible really shows its readers about things like, say, women, or teaching, or pastoring. More than that, I see more clearly who the God is in whose image I am created, and in whose image you are too. I've also begun to find the voice and the words Jesus has given me. It was still a surprise in 2019 when I became a pastor, though. Even now I shake my head at it.

A few years before becoming a pastor, I became a spiritual director. That development surprised me less. During my training to become one, I discovered that there were discernible patterns in my travels with Jesus and his book—patterns which other Jesus followers in other times and places and cultures have experienced too.[1] Some people call them stages of faith.[2] But— one of my colleagues in training protested as we were learning these things—is there anything *biblical* about these patterns? Where does it say in the Bible that our faith goes through stages?

At that point, even though I hadn't yet become a spiritual director or started working online with people who are deconstructing, which I do in conjunction with in-person pastoring, something about that protest ruffled me. I still believe the Bible is uniquely God's book, but I no longer see it as a manual for how to live. I take it more as a conversation with God about what God is like and how to reflect God's image most truly in the world. Also, I knew my own "stages" in walking with Jesus were real and true. So I started looking for the patterns of the saints within the Bible itself.

Here's the theory which, from observation and experience, undergirds this book: Getting to know God through the person of Jesus Christ happens over time, in narrative stages, just like any friendship does. But unlike any other friendship, the closer someone follows after Jesus—the better they get to know him— the better they will know, and eventually be, themselves. My working hypothesis for us as we go forward from here is that watching this following-for-transformation happen in someone else's story can enable it to happen more readily in our own.

If you've grown up in a church tradition where Bible studies were emphasized, you will quickly discover that this book is decidedly not a traditional Bible study, though it does incorporate biblical content, quoted or retold, on every page. The kind of transformative learning we're going for here is better caught than taught, as they say, so I will be *showing* what I've observed of Jesus through Peter's story, more than *telling* it. (We'll talk more about that in chapter 1.) At the end of each chapter, you'll have a chance to reflect on and interact with Jesus for yourself through spiritual practice, introspective questions, or an embodied process to help bring the chapter's conclusions home.

At the beginning of each chapter, under the title, I've shared the relevant Bible passages we'll be imaginatively engaging. If you are familiar with the Bible already and/or you have a complicated relationship with it because of how it's been wielded in your life before now, you can feel free to move directly into the chapter content. On the other hand, if this is your first encounter with these stories or you're the kind of person who likes to dig into the details—and maybe wants to evaluate my perspective for yourself—please feel free to look up these encounters in the Bible. Bible apps with various Bible translations are readily available, which will make finding the passages easy. With one significant exception in chapter two, any Bible quotes I use will be from the New International Version (NIV).

We can read enough about a few people in the Bible to see the patterns or stages of a relationship with God (Hebrew Bible/

Old Testament) or specifically with Jesus (New Testament). But I doubt there's anyone whose life more clearly demonstrates those stages than Simon Peter. At times, Peter gets held back by his community or tries to strike out independently of community. Ultimately, though, he discovers that, in a world without the visible presence of Jesus any longer, the best way to stay close to Jesus is in community with other people getting closer to Jesus and themselves. You're about to encounter—for the first or millionth time—the story of a man who started out believing one set of things about God and himself, then followed Jesus and discovered the truth. Which was never a set of beliefs, anyway, but a person—a life transformed into an image of God. May you discover that person more fully for yourself as you read this book.

CHAPTER 1

A NEW JOB AND A NEW NAME

John 1:35–42; Luke 5:1–11; Matthew 4:18–20

really thought I knew the disciple formerly known as Simon. If you're at all familiar with the New Testament, you probably think you do too. The man is chronically impulsive. Almost terminally foot-in-mouth. Earnest and emotional. I even wrote him that way in a novel.[3] But that was before I climbed into his story.

Maybe you and I weren't wrong, exactly, in our previous impressions. But getting to know a disciple through paying attention—not to application points or tiny episodes but to his own entire story—showed me that this disciple was much deeper and more complex than I first thought. Through immersing myself in the details of the biblical text and following Simon's own journey, what I found was a human being who discovered both God and himself through the person of Jesus. That discovery, in turn, helped me find more of God and myself. I have a hunch it could do the same for you.

Certainly Jesus's teachings helped Simon make sense of everything he was experiencing once he gave up fishing to follow a rabbi. But it was the story that changed him. I mean, the story he was living by being with Jesus—watching Jesus, interacting with Jesus, being loved by Jesus, and learning to love Jesus. Stories are, after all, how we humans learn best. Maybe that's because stories are who we are.

It seems a little weird that many if not most Western Christians come to our holy book, the Bible, as a book of almost anything else but stories by which to be changed. Most of the Bible is not rules and teaching—at least, not in the way we usually understand those terms. It's also not a science book, even though it describes (admittedly quite differently) some things that science also describes. It's not a psychology book, even though we can see human psychology in play all the way from Genesis through Revelation. It's not a history book, even though it is full of people who really lived and breathed and did crazy stuff, sometimes opposing the will of God and sometimes by the power of God. It's also not an instruction manual, even though both the Old and New Testaments contain sets of instructions.

Most of all, the Bible is a storybook.

Let me explain. When many people hear or say the word "story," they think "fiction," or "not true," or even "lie," but that's not what *story* in its truest sense means. Some stories are fiction. Some are nonfiction. Both kinds can be a way of telling the truth. They just tell it differently than, say, science or psychology or history—or rules—do. The Bible's stories all tell the truth— but they're still stories. That is, they are narratives with vibrant characters, discernible plotlines, conflicts, climaxes—all the elements of a good story. Some people, including the author of this book, would argue that the entire Bible itself is really one big story that is still being told.

Depending on who you ask (or which internet search links you click), only ten percent of our Bible could really be considered a rule book, but much teaching in many churches, as well as many Bible study materials, focuses on that ten percent. If that's the kind of church we're in or the background we came from, when we try to engage the stories, we are usually still thinking in terms of the ten percent. And so we wrestle principles out of the stories or poetry to "apply to our lives." This can be easier to do with some of the stories than others, and while looking for application is not a terrible exercise, what if the stories are primarily there for another reason? What if they mean to introduce us to people like us and to show what happens when those people do (or don't) merge their stories with God's? What if the stories are an invitation for us to do the same thing, and in the process to be changed? What if the change God hopes for is not for us to fill our heads with information or systematically check off a list of rules, but for us to encounter Jesus, the Word of God who is telling—and inhabiting—the Story?

My prayer for this book is that by the end of it, even though we won't cover every anecdote in the Bible about the disciple formerly known as Simon, we will feel like we've gotten a better sense of who he was. Even more importantly, though, I hope as we observe his experiences with Jesus, we will experience Jesus ourselves. We might not learn any new principles or easily stated applications, but I pray by the end of this book, we will all have "learned Jesus" in our souls a little bit more.

Now, let me tell you a story.

Simon is the responsible one. He is a family man with a fishing business to manage. His brother Andrew works with him sometimes. Andrew, clearly younger, doesn't feel the same responsibilities. He and his buddy John—also a younger brother in a fishing family—are spending more and more time running after some crazy prophet-preacher guy, John the Baptizer. Simon doesn't have time for that. He stays with the boats and the nets.

You know who Simon is—he's Jesus's friend Peter. We've already pegged him as loud and impulsive, which is to say . . . not the responsible one. But let's not jump ahead of the story. Right now, he's still Simon. And here in John 1—and Luke 5— and Matthew 4—we don't see impulsivity. It's Andrew, Simon's brother, who's gallivanting after a religious guru. In all three Gospel takes on this story of Simon meeting and coming to follow Jesus, Simon is working. Besides his younger brother, he has a wife. Her mother lives with them. We don't know if he and his wife have kids, but he has a decent-sized, if simple, house for a fisherman in Capernaum.[4] He's got to keep food on the table.

That's why it's Andrew who makes the introduction. Andrew and John have been following and learning from John the Baptizer for a while, so when one day the Baptizer points at a passerby and says, "Look! The Lamb of God!" (John 1:36), they evidently know what he's talking about—maybe because they heard him say it yesterday. In any case, they stop following the Baptizer around and start following "God's lamb" instead.

"Rabbi," they say to the man who John the Baptizer has pointed out, once he turns around and notices them, "Where are you staying?" (1:38).

To a person like me, who—for better or worse—comes from the dominant culture in the United States of America, this is a bizarre introduction. No sharing of names, as in, "Hi,

I'm Andrew and this is John." Not even, "Our former rabbi says you're the Lamb of God who takes away the sin of the world, so can we follow you instead?" They just immediately ask Jesus where he's staying, and then he invites them to spend time with him there. Which is maybe weird, too, because it possibly wasn't even his own house.

Many cultures worldwide are far more hospitable than mine. In white American culture, we want to get to know someone before we invite them to our house. (Also, it's usually our own house, or at least a place we're renting.) When I lived and worked among immigrants and refugees in England, however, I became quite adept at inviting myself over to visit my friends who had moved there from the opposite side of the globe. In this story, Andrew and John invite themselves over to where Jesus is staying. To be fair, Jesus himself kicks off the interaction. "What do you want?" (1:38) he asks, when he notices them following him. What they want, evidently, is to know him. We get to know each other best by entering one another's stories—and what better way to do that than to see where a person lives?

We're not told what these three talk about, but by the time they leave, in the span of only one afternoon, they have realized that Jesus is more than just another religious teacher—even more than their beloved Baptizer. "We have found the Messiah!" (John 1:41), Andrew crows to his brother when he gets home. Then, regardless of what Simon may have thought of it, he allows Andrew to drag him to Jesus.

Jesus takes one look at Simon and immediately renames him. "'You are Simon, son of John. You will be called Cephas (which, when translated, is Peter)" (John 1:42). We might note here that Jesus says, "You *will be called . . .*" as if this new name will only apply later. Simon is called Peter most of the time nowadays. But the nickname didn't stick right away.

Why would it have? Although it's possible, there's no evidence in the Bible itself that Simon has ever met Jesus before this. The fact that Andrew has to introduce them, and that John the Gospel writer tells us that Jesus just looks at Simon and renames him hints at this possibility. And yet here's this supposed Messiah, giving Simon a nickname at first sight. It's even kind of an affectionate nickname—the kind you give someone after you've known them well and for a while. The kind that both affirms some quality about them and knocks the bearer down a peg or two. We've been told that "Peter" means *rock*, but it's both arguable and—based on the other nicknames Jesus gives people—likely that the kind of rock *Peter* refers to isn't boulder-strong (and maybe pretentious) like, say, Dwayne "the Rock" Johnson. Peter's name still resonates strength but implies a smaller stone. Maybe something more like "Pebble," or "Rocky."

I think if I were Simon—I mean, Peter—the nickname would've felt random to me. Simon's a fisherman. He has nothing to do with pebbles, stones, rocks, boulders. There's a chance Jesus does, though. It turns out the biblical term traditionally translated *carpenter* when describing Jesus in the Gospels, doesn't necessarily mean woodworker. It might mean that. It might mean handyman. Or it might imply he was a stonecutter or a stonemason or maybe some other type of skilled craftsman.[5] Simon Peter doesn't know it yet, but his soul—which has just been named "Rocky"—is about to be shaped in the hands of a skilled artisan.

Now Simon and Jesus have met, but Simon, it appears, goes back to his boats and his nets and his family. He keeps on working at his trade. He doesn't plan to traipse after this rabbi as his brother seems to want him to. Simon hasn't spent enough time with Jesus yet to know one way or another if this is the Messiah. Let Andrew go if he wants. Simon has responsibilities.

On the other hand, the rabbi has moved into the neighborhood, and he seems like a good man, even if he is a little free with the nicknames. Simon doesn't mind letting this Jesus get into his boat to do his teaching. It doesn't hurt to help a rabbi in small ways. Sound travels better over water, and with the rabbi in the boat, the crowd of people gathering on the beach can't get too close and be distracting to the rabbi—or accidentally push him into the lake.

This morning, though, Simon is wrapping up a long night of fishing, or rather, of trying to fish. He's caught nothing. Rabbi Jesus is teaching from the moored boat, and Simon is cleaning the nets but not really paying attention. That's another reason we learn better from stories than lectures: unless people have a personal experience to attach the teaching to, many find lectures boring, and they won't remember the point. Simon is tuning the teaching out. To this day we don't know what, specifically, Jesus said from the boat that day. But he is about to give Simon a story—a personal experience. He wraps up his talk right around the time Simon's ready to pack everything in and get some rest. But he doesn't get out of the boat. He turns to Simon. "Put out into deep water, and let down the nets for a catch" (Luke 5:4), he says.

Have you ever had someone who doesn't know your job try to tell you how to do your job? If you have, you might know that

Simon, this guy who we tend to think was such a loudmouth, is pretty restrained in this case.

He doesn't say, "Jesus, you're not a fisherman. You don't know what you're talking about. We fish at night. We just got in. Everything's cleaned up and we're tired. Read the room. Maybe another time we'll take you out fishing if you want, okay?"

He does get a little passive aggressive, maybe, but can you blame him? "Master," he says, "we've worked hard all night and haven't caught anything. But *because you say so*, I will let down the nets" (Luke 5:5).[6]

And then the professional fisherman—who knew from having apprenticed with others and from his own personal experience that if they hadn't caught any fish last night, they weren't going to catch any this morning—gets schooled by a craftsman-rabbi. The nets fill up. The nets start to break. Simon—and presumably Andrew—have to call John and his older brother James to come help them haul in the catch so they don't lose it all. And then both boats start to sink.

The catch of fish is the story, but somehow in living that story, Simon Peter is hooked. He is never going to be the same again. I could tell you this for certain even if you didn't know anything else about Simon Peter and even if I didn't know anything else about Simon Peter. Do you know how I know he's never going to be the same? Because this is a divinely well-told story. If you took a creative writing class, you might have a teacher who would tell you that to write a good story you should "show, not tell." That's what Luke does here. He doesn't *say*, "and that was when Simon's life changed." He *shows* us.

In every verse where the disciple is named in Luke 5, Luke calls him "Simon." In Luke 5:3, he's called Simon. Verse four:

Simon. Verse five: Simon. Verse ten: Simon. But when the miracle happens, suddenly we get verse eight: "When Simon *Peter* saw this, he fell at Jesus's knees and said, 'Go away from me, Lord. I am a sinful man!'"

In the very instant that a skilled craftsman doubling as a holy man overturns the professional expectations of a fisherman, that fisherman discovers he does not know as much about himself and his world as he thought he did. As the boats start to sink, Simon's world turns upside-down, and he knows that he is in the presence of someone beyond his comprehension. His response to that realization, which he doesn't seem to have had when he was initially introduced to Jesus by his brother, is that he is a sinner, and by rights, he probably needs to get as far away from this soul craftsman as possible. Luke doesn't *tell* us any of that apart from the detail that all four fishermen are "astonished." And yet Luke *shows* us what happened by sharing the fisherman's kneeling confession and, more powerfully, in only one verse calling the fisherman "Simon *Peter.*" That, he shows us, is the moment when Simon begins to be transformed into "Rocky."

Verse ten goes back to calling Peter "Simon," and I suspect that's because this is only the beginning of his story. When Jesus calls us to follow him, he is really calling us to become somebody new, and simultaneously somebody we were always intended to be. It takes a little while sometimes to shake off our old self and our old ways so we can become our true self. But verse eight is the clue that Peter has begun that transition. And Jesus comforts him as Peter stands at the brink: "Don't be afraid" (Luke 5:10).

Jesus doesn't say, "You sure are a sinner! Get out of my sight. Oh, and I'm keeping the boat."

He doesn't say, "I'm glad you've realized how sinful you are. Let me itemize everything that's wrong with you so we can work on it together. Let me remind you of what it means to be obedient to God."

It's more like Jesus says, "You think staying away from me is the solution to your sinfulness? How about you spend time with me instead? Follow me. I have a job for you to do. It's kind of like the one you've been doing all your life, only different. Instead of netting fish, I want you to help me catch other souls, just like I caught yours. I've got you, Rocky."

"Then Jesus said to Simon, 'Don't be afraid; from now on you will fish for people.' So they [all four of those guys, according to Matthew] pulled their boats up on shore [for the second time that morning], left everything and followed him" (Luke 5:10–11).

The end.

Just kidding. This is only the beginning—for Peter, and maybe for us too. Peter knows all about fishing for fish. Or at least, he thought he did. He's about to find out what happens when you invite Jesus into your day-to-day life—not just into the things you struggle to do, but the things you're so good at you don't even have to think about them. He's about to discover what it means to fish for people.

FOLLOW MORE CLOSELY

Find an outdoor location that relaxes you and take a walk. Think about your day-to-day activities. What are you so good at you take it for granted or take pride in it? Imagine and write down some ways that Jesus could reframe that skill, like he reframed fishing for Peter. Would the reframe bring you closer to Jesus or make him harder to reach? Ask Jesus if he has a nickname for you, and if he'll let you know what it is. Spend some time in silence allowing Jesus to pay attention to you. How does it feel?

CHAPTER 2

GONE FISHING

Luke 10:1–24

I got my first Bible when I was six years old, and I thought it was a fine gift. By the time I turned seven, I was a decent reader, so I could get through most of Genesis (there were a couple of passages in there that baffled me, but it wasn't too bad) and up to chapter 20 in Exodus, where the Ten Commandments show up. After that I got stuck. I spent most of the rest of my childhood going to church and Christian school, consequently going through occasional spurts of trying to read the Bible but not necessarily being terribly motivated to do it, and mostly feeling kind of bored and lost by it.

In my early teens, I had a conversation with my dad about this. He had been a missionary, was a pastor at the time, and is now retired in the way that good lifelong pastors retire, which means no longer getting paid to do the same things they've done their entire adult lives. I wanted to want to read the Bible, but it was too hard, I told him. If I managed not to zone out completely, what happened was questions. Lots of questions. I didn't know what to do with all the questions, because the Bible isn't like the math books I grew up with, which had easy-to-find answers in the back. On the contrary, the back is one of the most confusing parts of the whole thing.

"Well," my dad said, "why don't you get yourself a notebook, and when you read your Bible, you can write down your questions. And then one of these days you and I can sit down together and talk about them."

I have since been told by lots of people that church is not a safe place for questions, and every time someone tells me that, I feel sad and a little confused because my dad was my pastor growing up, and he was a safe place for questions. Also, that one piece of advice he gave me—to write down my questions—keeps teaching me how to read the Bible. I don't know that my dad and I ever really ended up having that sit-down to discuss all the questions, but it was comforting and even affirming to know that we could have. Maybe one reason we didn't was because after a while I started writing my questions as if I were talking directly to God, instead of as if I were going to bring them to my dad. In this way reading the Bible became—and continues to be—like having an ongoing conversation with God over decades.

All these years later, I find myself following in my dad's footsteps as a pastor, and so maybe not surprisingly, one of the things I feel called to do in that role is to help people learn to read the Bible better. You may be a more faithful Bible reader than I am, building your relationship with God through Scripture for longer than I have. Then again, you may have been genuinely wounded by misuse of the "double-edged sword" (Hebrews 4:12), and my hunch is that even more of us still feel about the Bible the way I did as a kid: stuck.

As I said earlier, most of the Bible is a storybook. A *true* storybook. The thing about stories is that you might not understand everything in every story right away or all the time. But while it helps to have people in your life who have learned the original languages and studied the Bible in depth to teach and guide what you're reading, you really don't need a degree in science or math or psychology or even literature or theology to get something out of a story. Especially when it's a story that God wants to tell you already.

I believe that the same story God is telling through the Bible is the one God is trying to tell through you and me—through our own individual and collective lives. We are participants in the same story these people in the Bible inhabited. I hope your reading of the Hebrew and Christian Scriptures turns into a conversation with God about yourself and these people who preceded you, which turns into a deeper relationship with God than you've known before. I also hope that you'll find yourself in Simon Peter's story and from there see a way forward as you continue to put one foot in front of the other in your pursuit of Jesus, who loves you. Maybe the most surprising thing will be how you discover yourself in the process.

I hope all this for you even when Simon Peter isn't specifically named in the story we're looking at. Because today he isn't, but all the same, I think this chapter's reading experiment is the best entry point for finding yourself in his story. Also, it's the best episode to carry us forward from Chapter 1, because here we discover what his new job really looked like. Here we see how a person goes about fishing for people. However, because Simon Peter himself isn't named in the story, you get to write the rest of this chapter. Don't be nervous. You don't have to prepare ahead of time. You just need to read a story, and then join in.

At the beginning of Luke 9, Jesus sends his twelve male disciples fishing—but not literally. The metaphor is just another way to describe telling people about the Kingdom of God. Not all of the Twelve were professional fishermen—probably just the four we've already met: Simon Peter, Andrew, James, and John. Maybe this gave them a head start. Or maybe Jesus had other job-related analogies for the same thing that worked with the other guys. For example, he starts his instructions in our focus passage with a harvest metaphor and doesn't mention fishing at all. But we're following Jesus by following Peter in this book, so for this chapter we'll keep our guy's "fishing for people" metaphor.

After the Twelve go out to tell people that the Kingdom of God is coming right up, Jesus sends out "seventy-two others." This group most likely included Jesus's women disciples whom Luke mentions in his chapter 8,[7] which is another reason for us to look at this story at the beginning of our sojourn with Jesus and Peter. It's not within the scope of this book to address what it is like specifically to be a woman who follows Jesus. We're looking at the process in the story of a man because frankly, the Bible really does give us more information about male characters generally than about female ones. Fortunately, Peter's story has real overlap for real people of any demographic. But as we set out with him, it's nice to be able to enter the journey with a more diverse crowd, in which there could be someone much more specifically like you or me. In fact, today there is.

As Luke tells the story, we're in a crowd who were not all men and may not even all have been adults, but most of whom probably weren't professional fishermen either. It doesn't matter. We're all going people-fishing together as we explore Luke 10.

Luke places this story right after an account of some people who offered to follow Jesus but evidently weren't willing to make the personal sacrifices involved. (Bible writers don't always tell their stories in chronological order, because they're usually trying to communicate other true things besides accurate timelines.) By his story placement, Luke wants us to notice that Jesus has just made the point that following him—which, from our perspective in this book, Simon Peter just decided to do a chapter ago—is no joke. It's a commitment, and Jesus expects it to take priority over all our other responsibilities and relationships. Knowing that makes some people leave in chapter 9. But Jesus still has at least seventy-two people sticking around who somehow think this is worth it. It's still early in Jesus's ministry. These seventy-two don't all know for sure who he is. None of them know where Jesus is heading—even if they might think they do. Yet they are still following.

Keep this background in mind as you read the passage below. Read it slowly. Even better, read it three or more times. After a while, if you have an imagination that works this way, imagine that you are Simon Peter. Your life started when Jesus got into your boat and overturned your expectations of the world and your understanding of yourself. Then he told you that you would help him fish for people. He's already sent you out with eleven of his other friends to start soul-fishing, and now you're off with this bigger group. Even while heading out to tell people about God's Kingdom while Jesus stays behind, you find yourself learning about Jesus. You learn even more as he debriefs you when you get back.

If you struggle to activate your mind's eye this way—or if you find yourself uncomfortable with identifying with a male from the Bible's dominant culture for now—either imagine yourself as another follower who fits your demographic better, or simply notice which words and phrases stand out to you as you read. Why are you noticing them? What are you feeling in your body when you notice them? Write the words down. You will still be able to engage with our questions afterward.

In most of this book, when I directly quote from the Bible, I use the New International Version because it's familiar to a lot of people, including me. In this case, though, for the very same reason, we'll be reading the story in its entirety from the *Kingdom New Testament*, a translation by N.T. Wright. A slightly less familiar translation should help you notice things in the story which you might not notice otherwise.

> After this the master commissioned seventy others, and sent them ahead of him in pairs to every town and place where he was intending to come.
>
> 'There's a great harvest out there,' he said to them, 'but there aren't many workers. So plead with the harvest-master to send out workers for the harvest.
>
> 'Off you go now. Remember, I'm sending you out like lambs among wolves. Take no money-bag, no pack, no sandals—and don't stop to pass the time with anyone on the road. Whenever you go into a house, first say, "Peace on this house." If a child of peace lives there, your peace will rest on them; but if not, it will return to you.
>
> 'Stay in the same house, and eat and drink what they provide. The worker deserves to be paid, you see. Don't go from house to house. If you go into a town and they welcome you, eat what is provided, heal the

sick who are there, and say to them, "God's kingdom has come close to you." But if you go into a town and they don't welcome you, go out into the streets of the town and say, "Here is the very dust of your town clinging to our feet—and we're wiping it off in front of your eyes! But you should know this: God's kingdom has come close to you!" Let me tell you, on that day it will be more tolerable for Sodom than for that town.

'Woe betide you, Chorazin! Woe betide you, Bethsaida! If the powerful deeds done in you had been done in Tyre and Sidon, they would have repented long ago, sitting in sackcloth and ashes. But it will be more tolerable for Tyre and Sidon in the judgment than for you. And you, Capernaum—you want to be lifted up to heaven, do you? No: you'll be sent down to Hades!

'Anyone who hears you, hears me; anyone who rejects you, rejects me; and anyone who rejects me, rejects the one who sent me.'

The seventy came back exhilarated.

'Master,' they said, 'even the demons obey us in your name!'

'I saw the satan fall like lightning from heaven,' he replied. 'Look: I've given you authority to tread on snakes and scorpions, and over every power of the enemy. Nothing will ever be able to harm you. But— don't celebrate having spirits under your authority. Celebrate this, that your names are written in heaven.'

Then and there Jesus celebrated in the holy spirit.

'I thank you, father,' he said, 'Lord of heaven and earth! You hid these things from the wise and intelligent, and revealed them to babies. Yes, father, that was what you graciously decided. Everything has been given me by my father. Nobody knows who the son is except the father, and nobody knows who the father is except the son, and anyone to whom the son wishes to reveal him.'

Jesus then turned to the disciples privately.

'A blessing on the eyes,' he said, 'which see what you see! Let me tell you, many prophets and kings wanted to see what you see, and they didn't see it; and to hear what you hear, and they didn't hear it!'[8]

This was quite the fishing trip. I'm not sure even the most exciting deep sea tuna catch could match it for cosmic upheaval. We've just gotten a backstage glimpse at something of the new order that Jesus came to bring—not on his own, but through his followers. Somehow, our fishing trip for people has shaken the heavens, and we have more authority than we ever knew. So does Simon Peter. But even though he's experienced demons submitting to him in Jesus's name more than once now, he doesn't even know the half of who Jesus is or of who he himself is becoming.

FOLLOW MORE CLOSELY

Here's where you can write the rest of the chapter. Unpack what you experienced as you read the passage in a less familiar version. What was happening in the story from your perspective? Who was your ministry partner? How did you feel about that person? What did you feel about the different things that Jesus instructed you to do and not do? Did you enjoy going and staying with people you don't know? How did you feel when you completed your task and reported back to Jesus? What did he say that sounded exciting or encouraging? What did you like or agree with? What made you feel uncomfortable or challenged you? What questions do you have?

Don't be afraid of misinterpreting or of asking a stupid question. Misinterpretation is really difficult to do with this way of reading the Bible, and chances are if you have the question, so does someone else. If you're so inclined, invite a friend with whom you can bat your insights around—and then go for it!

CHAPTER 3

IF IT'S YOU

Matthew 14:13–33

'm pretty sure I was less distractible before social media than I am now. With so many avenues for input, I have a really hard time focusing these days. But focus matters. It gives us direction. What we focus on reveals where we're placing our faith—our trust, our reliance. And where we place our faith affects who we become—our identity.

Putting focus on and faith in ourselves alone is a dead end, since our identity is formed by whom or what we trust. If we trust in ourselves before we know ourselves, we become a closed loop and don't mature very well. Despite how such vulnerability leaves us open to the potential for harmful input, we do need other people to help us figure out who we are. If we focus on and learn to trust someone or something outside ourselves—provided that person's identity is healthily developed and secure—our own identity will form much more readily. Then we will become people of substance who are reliable and worth trusting. Let's see what happens to Simon—and to us—as we focus on the next part of his story.

"When Jesus heard what had happened . . ." Matthew says (Matthew 14:13). Which might, if you are a vigilant and curious reader, make you ask, "Okay. So, *what had happened*?"

We know that the Gospels often tell the same stories with different details from each other. We also know that one of the details they occasionally change is the order in which they tell the stories. Lots of times the actual order of events—which we, in our time and culture, tend to think is very important—was less significant to these writers than the themes they were trying to emphasize.

For example, it's mostly unclear whether the last chapter's story about the seventy-two happened before or after today's story. Because of the fact that none of the Gospel writers make it a point to always tell every single story in chronological order, when the Gospels do match the order of events in their telling, there's something significant for us to consider in the chronological order itself. All four Gospel writers match the order of at least two events leading up to today's story.

The matching "what had happened" that Jesus hears about is that his cousin John the Baptizer, whom we met in chapter one, has been executed. The Baptizer had described Jesus as "the Lamb of God, who takes away the sin of the world" (John 1:29). He had described himself with a verse from the Old Testament prophet Isaiah: "The voice of one calling in the wilderness, 'Make straight the way for the Lord'" (John 1:23). Making straight the way for the Lord got him into some hot water with a local pseudo-king, Herod, and he ended up in prison.

While John was in prison, Jesus sent his twelve disciples (at least two of whom, as we have seen, used to be the Baptizer's disciples) also to prepare the way of the Lord in the towns Jesus

hadn't visited yet. As we saw in the last chapter, they were to go
and teach people about the Kingdom of God and heal the sick,
just as Jesus was doing, getting people ready for Jesus to come
visit them himself. When we pick the story up here in Matthew
14, the Twelve have just come back from their mission trip, and
Jesus is getting the news that his faithful cousin has been unjustly
beheaded.

So Matthew tells us, "When Jesus heard what had happened,
he withdrew by boat privately to a solitary place" (Matthew
14:13). Here's why it's a good idea to read the same story in all
four Gospels if you can. Mark, Luke, and John also mention the
death of John the Baptist, but they focus more on the disciples'
return from their trip. When we read this story in those Gospels,
the emphasis can make us think, "Oh, how nice of Jesus—who
has obviously just been sitting around doing nothing while the
Twelve are gone—to try to take his faithful disciples on a little
debriefing retreat." If we're familiar with the story, we know he
doesn't succeed—there's a crowd of people coming right up—but
it's a thoughtful impulse, right?

Matthew, on the other hand, focuses on Jesus. "When Jesus
heard what had happened"—that his cousin, the one biological
family member that we know of who truly believed in him at this
point—had been executed, he got in a boat with the other people
who had just been preparing the way of the Lord. Matthew
doesn't mention the Twelve in the boat, although we can be sure
they were there. It was probably Simon Peter's boat, in fact. And
Jesus wasn't part of the crew.

What if the real reason—or at least a big reason—Jesus
wanted to take the boat and his disciples to a quiet place was that

he was grieving? What if it was that he knew he was ultimately going to face something even worse than his cousin had? And so maybe he wanted a chance to connect with his Father and with this band of brothers he was building for himself. They hadn't been with him when he got the news because they were off doing the work he had given them. What if he—as much as or even more than the Twelve—was the one who needed the support and the debriefing right then? Jesus is God. And he is also human. When we are at our lowest, we humans need God. And we need each other.

The Twelve get back from their first trip exhilarated, and there's Jesus waiting for them. But his face is drawn, his eyes are tired, and he says, "Hey guys, let's take the boat and go to that place—you know the one." Maybe it was a place they had retreated to before, where Jesus had taught them and they had learned what they needed to know for their trip. It's clear that the intention now for this boat trip is for everybody to get a little R&R. Matthew says, "He *withdrew* by boat *privately* to a *solitary* place" (14:13), and later in verse 15 the disciples say, "This is a *remote place*." In other words, this place is in the middle of nowhere. You get the idea that nobody else is supposed to know about it.

So you can almost *feel* the exhausted, disappointed, but maybe slightly hilarious surprise that Matthew shows-but-doesn't-tell us: Jesus withdrew. Privately. To a solitary place . . . "*Hearing of this*, the crowds followed him on foot from the town"!

Just think about this for a second. The Twelve went off to prepare the way for Jesus. Suddenly there are a whole lot more people than there were before who know about Jesus. And we don't get the impression anywhere that every—or any—of these disciples was a strategist, or had high emotional intelligence, or even was the sharpest tack in the box, so perhaps somebody on their Kingdom-declaring trip spilled the beans about this location. Maybe more than one of them did. Maybe it was Peter. There would have been no ill intent. They were all excited about Jesus and what he was asking them to do. They wanted other people to get to know him too. And they had been tasked with preparing the way. So they did . . . possibly all the way to the remote solitary place.

Maybe that's why Jesus doesn't turn the boat around. For various reasons, every person on it including Jesus is exhausted. But Matthew tells us, "When Jesus landed and saw a *large* crowd, *he had compassion on them* and healed their sick" (Matthew 14:14). Then he feeds them all-you-can-eat fish and chips from almost nothing. He knows these people are the reason he came to that time and place. Even though they don't really understand who he is, there is something about him they know they need. They seek him out, and he lets them find him. In the book of the Hebrew prophet Jeremiah, God tells God's people, "You will seek me and find me when you seek me with all your heart. I will be found by you, declares the LORD" (Jeremiah 29:13–14).

We won't spend a lot of time here focusing on the eating part of the story except to point out that in this instance, Jesus does fulfill a hint of Jeremiah's promise, and he does it when, humanly speaking, he's running on empty. We don't often think of this story this way. We know the disciples have already spent a significant time traveling and healing people, and so they're tired, but we can kind of imagine them pushing through just a little bit longer because now Jesus is here and they can default to him. And Jesus *is* here and they *can* rely on him—they do that and miracles happen—but Jesus is sad and also tired. Most of us get tired when we're sad too. Keeping all that in mind will help us have a clearer imagination for the rest of the story, which is where we are about to focus.

Specifically, we're focusing on the part after Jesus says to the Twelve, "Okay guys—take the boat and get out of here. I'll catch up with you later" and after he gets the crowds to leave too. Matthew says he dismissed them, John says he hid from them. We can guess it was a bit of both. It's two different ways of expressing the idea that *finally* Jesus gets his alone time in this solitary, middle of nowhere place, with his Father. We can tell how restorative this time is for Jesus, because afterward, he walks on the water to his friends.

People have proposed varying theories about the significance of Jesus's walking on the water. Some people talk about Mark (who most likely got the bulk of information for his Gospel from Peter) highlighting connections to the Exodus story.[9] Others suggest that this episode is about Jesus's displaying his authority over the supernatural powers that oppose God, which are often represented by storms and seas.[10] I see the dynamic of Jesus displaying his authority over the supernatural powers more evidently in the story where Jesus calms a truly life-threatening storm on the sea of Galilee (Matthew 8:23–27, Mark 4:35–41, Luke 8:22–25). In our present story, the wind is kicked up and the waves are choppy, but it doesn't seem like anyone is in fear of their lives. I wonder if sometimes (certainly not always) the deeper underlying symbolism of Jesus's action at any given time had more to do with who he is by nature and less the point he was consciously making in the moment.

I propose that consciously, walking on water is Jesus's version of letting his hair down. Otherwise, what is the point of this miracle? On a ministry, spiritual, or even logistical level, there is no real purpose to what happens here. Jesus doesn't have to walk on the water to get to his disciples. He could walk on the land and meet them in the morning. Or he could stay where he is and have the disciples come pick him up later. He's not trying to prove anything to crowds—they're all gone for the night.

Picture Jesus, alone with his Father, being comforted and strengthened. Staring across the wave-tossed Sea of Galilee. Feeling the wind that's tossing the waves which are spraying his face, blowing through his hair. He takes a deep breath of it. Coincidentally (or not), the Hebrew word for wind and breath is the same word used for spirit. We could say that nobody's around except Jesus, his Father, and his Spirit—and those twelve friends of his are way out there in their little boat, wrestling with this same wind as they try to get to the other side of the lake. After an exhausting day of compassion and giving, after the news of the unjust execution of his cousin, Jesus is free to be totally himself. He smiles. He takes a step onto the water and begins to walk. Jesus is having fun!

Sometimes people try to tell me Jesus was a big show-off and the only reason he did miracles was to get famous. But that doesn't add up. Healing people, if you can heal people, is not showing off. It's doing good. If you can do it, you should do it, whether you are a doctor, trained and operating according to natural laws, or whether you have a supernatural ability from God. Jesus did not do flashy, show-off miracles. He healed people. This walking-on-water miracle, on the other hand, would be a flashy, show-off miracle—except no one else witnesses it except the Twelve. And here's how we know Jesus wasn't in the habit of doing things like this to show off: the disciples don't recognize him.

They see him coming across the water. He's too far away for them to see his features, and they don't say, "Oh hey look— it's Jesus. He's always doing stuff like that." No. Like me, and I assume you, they've never seen a human being walk on water before. They think he's a ghost. And they absolutely flip out.

Matthew says they "cried out in fear" (Matthew 14:26), but I think that's probably an understatement because remember, Jesus is not close enough for them to recognize him, and it's super windy out there, so it must be noisy, but Jesus still hears them. And then—maybe partly because he's experienced in preaching across the water from boats—he's able to call back loudly enough for them to hear him: "Chill, guys. It's me. Don't freak out." And now, finally, we get to Peter.

Two chapters ago, we saw a responsible working man named Simon begin to be transformed into the enthusiastic, impulsive, Jesus-devoted Peter that we know and love. I'm convinced that this is the story where those true colors really begin to shine through—where we see Peter being transformed by Jesus into who he truly is. "Lord, if it's you," he calls out to Jesus, "tell me to come to you on the water" (Matthew 14:28).

Before the giant catch of fish that we talked about, I doubt that guy *Simon* would ever have thought of suggesting he get out of his own boat (or anyone else's for that matter) when it was in the middle of a lake. (To clarify—the so-called "Sea of Galilee" is actually a really large lake, also known as Kinneret.) He would have known that the world just plain doesn't work like that. But after the catch of fish—another potentially showy miracle which only Simon and probably three other fishermen saw—his expectations of how the world works, at least around Jesus, have been overturned. And since then, this man *Peter* has been spending time with Jesus and becoming more like Jesus—to the point of having just gotten back from a trip where he was teaching and healing and even casting out demons like Jesus.

Two things seem to be going on in Peter's somewhat impulsive shout. The first is that he has discovered beyond the shadow of a doubt that wherever Jesus is, he wants to be. And—except for this long exhausting day they've all been through where none of them have really had a chance to reconnect with each other, and which has metaphorically felt a little like trying to row this boat back across the lake into the headwind—he hasn't had much opportunity to be with Jesus lately. So if it's really Jesus, he doesn't want to waste any more time apart from this man who has redefined his life and his world.

Also—and I suspect this was more intuitive than reasoned out—he's come back from doing all these amazing things that are just like what Jesus does (healing sick people and casting out demons, mainly). Now here's Jesus, walking on water. So "if it's really you, Jesus, and I can now do the things you can do, I can walk on water too." If it's not really Jesus, and Peter steps out of the boat, he's still close enough to the boat—and don't forget, he's familiar with water, he can swim—that the other disciples can haul him back in. But if it is Jesus, then because it's Jesus, Peter will be able to do this, and he doesn't want to miss another minute away from him. This is great faith and great love.

Sometimes people—I admit to once having been one of those people—like to make fun of Peter for being a little bit headlong and stupid, but what he does here is about his relationship with his Lord. *He loves Jesus.* The world will tell us that's stupid, certainly. The Bible calls it the "foolishness of God" (1 Corinthians 1:25). Which is the Bible's way of saying it's really the smartest thing we could ever do with our lives. Maybe, really, Peter was the smartest disciple.

Anyway, Jesus sees Peter's desire and loves it—and loves Peter—and invites Peter to join him, just as Peter asked. It is really him, after all. Jesus is not the one who says, "Hold up. You might want to think about this first. It is really me, but why don't you just sit tight, and I'll finish my walk to you. Leave this to the professional. Don't try this at home. Or in the middle of the Sea of Galilee." On the contrary, Jesus is restored and refreshed. Jesus is being fully himself with his Father and his twelve buddies, and he's having fun. This wind is nothing to him. Or it's the Spirit, which is even better. So—Peter wants to join in on the fun? Absolutely! "Come on then," says Jesus.

Peter gets out of the boat, and he doesn't sink, but at this point he must not even be thinking about that, because he's just focused on getting to Jesus and not on precisely how he's getting to him. My husband and I rehashed this story together the first time I taught it, and it was he who pointed out to me that Jesus must have still been a good distance away from the boat, since even though they could hear him, the disciples (including Peter) couldn't recognize him by sight. But also, my husband reasoned, this must have been true because when Peter starts to sink, the boat and the disciples aren't, after all, right there to haul him in.

Peter is focused on the figure standing on the waves, and Peter is walking. And he's walking and he's walking and he's walking, and he gets a decent way out, and he's almost to Jesus, and it really *is* Jesus (which he already knew, because he made it out there, but now he can see Jesus's face), and he smiles. And he looks around. "Yeah! I did it!" Only now he's not looking at Jesus anymore.

Maybe he's instinctively taking credit for having gotten out there—forgetting that it's only because of Jesus he's able to do such a thing—just like it was only because of Jesus that they were able to feed at least ten thousand people earlier that day. But whether he's taking personal credit or not, Peter is now focused on his surroundings, not Jesus. He's in the middle of a large body of water. It's a familiar body of water, but usually there's a boat between him and it. And the water is not, shall we say, like glass. It's windy out there. Also, by the way, people can't walk on water, which he maybe should've thought about before, because that giant wave just smacked him in the face and "Help!" He's sinking!

The boat is way back there. But Jesus is in front of him. As soon as Peter cries out, Jesus reaches out his hand and hauls Peter up. He doesn't wait. He doesn't choose to let Peter flounder a bit. Jesus *wants* his followers to imitate him. But maintaining that imitation takes focused faith in the one we're imitating. This is why I don't think anymore that—even though I used to—when Jesus says, "You of little faith, why did you doubt?" (Matthew 14:31), he says it in a stern, scolding tone. Maybe he was even grinning. "You asked if it was me, and it was, and you got all the way out here focused on me. Why did you stop?"

All the way back to the boat, Peter has his hand in Jesus's like Peter is a little kid. Which, as a follower of Jesus, he kind of is. They make their way back to the others through the wind and the waves, which don't die down until after they get into the boat. At which point, none of the other guys can do much else but worship Jesus. And that is the story of how the shenanigans of two friends almost ended—but didn't—in disaster.

Which is, I guess, the way we could look at it if we weren't focusing on Jesus. But it's really the story of focus and faith and identity. Simon began to transform into Peter the moment more fish than he had ever caught in his life landed in his boat. At first he thought the correct response to this Jesus, for whom the world worked differently than for anyone else, was to send him away. But Jesus showed Peter that really, the solution for his earthbound thoughts and behaviors was for Peter to spend *more* time with him, not less.

Peter took this seriously. Seriously enough to keep navigating the boat to shore even when they could clearly see that, instead of a solitary place, they were about to encounter all at once the crowds of people the twelve of them had been reaching out to for weeks before. He got through that day because his focus was on Jesus.

Peter takes spending time with Jesus seriously enough that when Jesus is just kind of messing around with the laws of physics for fun, Peter wants to be with him for that too. Work *and* play—everything in Peter's life is becoming focused on Jesus. And Peter's whole identity is changing because of it. He used to be a fisherman. Now he is fishing for people. Now he is supernaturally healing people and casting out demons. Now he is helping feed a crowd of far more people than even that giant catch of fish would have provided for—with a couple of pieces of bread and some sardines. Now he is walking on water. This is not who Simon was. But it is who Peter is becoming. He is becoming like the one he is focused on, in whom he has put his faith.

When Jesus caught Peter up out of the waves, he asked Peter why he doubted. I'm starting to think that doubt is not really so much disbelief as it is a shift of focus, and a shift of faith. While Peter was walking out to Jesus, he was focused on Jesus as he had been all day, but once he got there, he was distracted by what was around him. We all do this, don't we? Sometimes we say, "If only God would show up right in front of me, I would do this, or believe this" or whatever. And then we're distracted by shiny things or squirrels or social media. God couldn't have been *more* right in front of Peter than he was at that moment, and Peter loved Jesus and was being transformed into Jesus's likeness, and he *still* got distracted.

We don't have to beat ourselves up when we get distracted. Jesus doesn't. He refocuses us. He reminds us to trust him. He keeps on crafting our souls so that we reflect him—the glory of God. In other words, when we get tired, when we get distracted, when we get scared, Jesus doesn't usually take us out of our circumstances. He just grabs us by the hand and says, "Come on. You know me. Trust me."

It always helps, though, when we have a clearer idea of who he is. We—and Peter—are about to get one.

FOLLOW MORE CLOSELY

What are the winds and the waves that are buffeting you today—or most recently? What are you focusing on to get you through it? Is it working? Take some time to get outside and take a walk.

Imagine that Jesus is just ahead of you and that you are following him. Notice what the walk is like as you do this. What distracts you? Are you able to maintain your focus? What is it like when you do? Do you find your mind wandering to your "wind and waves"? How does Jesus bring your focus back to him? What does he say to you? What do you say to him?

CHAPTER 4

WHAT'S IN A NAME?

Matthew 16:13–28; Luke 9:18–27

We all want to find out who we really are, don't we? Many if not most of us spend our lives trying to figure it out, and once we think we've done that, we spend a lot of time trying to prove it to ourselves and other people. Me, for example? I was all hung up for a long time on the meaning of my name.

I'm told that I was almost named "Lisa" or "Astrid." Instead I ended up with Jennifer, the most popular girl's name in the United States from 1970 to 1984. In my middle school years when I was trying to forge my own unique identity as middle schoolers everywhere seem to do, I felt like my name was holding me back. Not only was it far too common, but I learned that it means "White wave" or "White phantom," not "Gracious lady" or whatever I had previously been told it meant. Then I found out that "Jennifer" is a derivative of "Guinevere," which is the name of King Arthur's wife. So that was cool—until I learned that she was an adulteress. I'm okay with my name now, but it took me a while to get there. Like many adolescents, I wasn't very happy with much about myself, to be honest.

Then I discovered Revelation 2:17. In it, Jesus says, "To the one who is victorious, I will give some of the hidden manna. *I will also give that person a white stone with a new name written on it, known only to the one who receives it.*" That bit about the white stone with the new name captivated me. I really wanted that stone! I really wanted to know what my true name was!

Reading that verse in Revelation as a kid was my first realization that not only does Jesus know everything about me, but ultimately, he knows my name. My real name—who I am—which, it turns out, comes straight from him. In fact, he gives me my name, my identity, and even though I still don't yet fully know what's written on that stone, one day I will. For now, I'm getting closer. I'm being fitted to it. He knows your name too. But he also wants to know who we think he is. What name do we give him?

We already know that Simon's story starts with a name: Simon, to begin with. Simon, son of Jonah. Simon, brother of Andrew. Simon the fisherman. Then Jesus came along and named him Peter—Rocky. It was shortly after that, through a semi-private but miraculous catch of fish, that Simon really began to be transformed into Peter. When Jesus captivated him, he told Peter he was going to make him a "fisher of men" instead of a fisher of fish. We've seen how Peter went out with the other eleven disciples (and later with a mixed group of 72 disciples), preparing the way for Jesus to come visit other towns. The preparation happened through Peter and the others doing what Jesus was doing. Proclaiming the Kingdom like Jesus. Healing like Jesus. Casting out demons like Jesus. Feeding people like Jesus. We've even seen Peter identify so closely with Jesus that, when Jesus was his focus, he could walk on the water like Jesus. Our vision, our focus, determines our identity.

Now Jesus is again with his core group of disciples. We don't know exactly when this story occurs in relation to the last chapter's—which means that's not a particularly important detail. But we do know that by now we have the feeding of the multitudes under our belts. We've already walked on water. We also remember that Jesus's cousin John the Baptizer has been beheaded. It's likely that Jesus is still grieving this as well as the knowledge that he is heading toward a much greater suffering.

Last time we saw Peter, Jesus and his disciples were having a hard time getting away for some R&R, but now it sounds like they're finally getting a little. Both Matthew and Mark tell us Jesus and the Twelve are traveling and arrive at Caesarea Philippi. Maybe it wasn't totally implausible to go to Caesarea Philippi for refreshment, as it was a known spiritual center, but it does seem like an unusual place for Jesus and his disciples to seek out for the purpose. The city had a waterfall and a cave associated with pagan deities—in Jesus's time, specifically Pan—and so for a Jewish rabbi and his Jewish apprentices, it could not have been particularly spiritually refreshing.

In fact, perhaps the refreshment was more physical and a withdrawal from people, though engaging Jesus's mission and identity on a deeper, more hidden level. The human crowds are gone, but Jesus is still investing in his disciples. It's Luke who tells us that Jesus was praying right before the conversation that we're about to listen in on. Luke says, "Once when Jesus was praying *in private* and his disciples were *with him* . . ." (Luke 9:18), which is a weird sentence if you think about it.

It might, though, remind us a bit of Matthew's saying, "Jesus withdrew privately to a solitary place," when we know the disciples were in the boat too. Apparently, Jesus and the Twelve are so tight at this point that Jesus feels relaxed with them. They often get portrayed as a bunch of buffoons, but evidently they are not a drain on his energy. It sounds like they are a support, and for him, being with them is as good as "being in private." He feels free to speak to his Father even when they're around.

So maybe Jesus is praying while they're walking to Caesarea Philippi, or maybe they get there and park themselves in a secluded place for a while, and Jesus prays there. Either way, maybe he is remembering the time when even his cousin John wasn't sure who Jesus was. Or thinking about his biological half-brothers in Nazareth who still don't believe in him. Or maybe he is considering the spiritual entities who have set up shop in the region they have just entered. Whatever is on his mind, suddenly he turns to his disciples and says, "All those people we were just with—all those people you guys were working with a couple of weeks ago on your trip—who do they say the Son of Man is?"

The disciples throw out some of the things they've heard. The hearsay hypotheses are a bit bizarre, because they seem to imply some kind of reincarnation idea that isn't part of Judaism. The idea that Jesus is his recently beheaded cousin is the weakest: Jesus was already doing ministry while John the Baptizer was still alive. It's possible, though, that people thought John had passed along a portion of his spirit to Jesus after he (John) was put in prison, like Elijah passed on a portion of his to Elisha in the First Testament[11] (2 Kings 2:9–14). Jesus listens to all the guesses that his disciples report back to him. Then he directs his question a little closer to home. "What about you guys?" he asks. "Who do *you* say I am?"

Jesus wants to be known too. And this makes sense. Jesus is God, and Jesus is somehow also human. Not half and half, either, like some of the entities the surrounding nations venerated. All and all. Way back in Exodus, when Moses asks God what God's name is, God answers, *I AM*. God himself is essence. He is existence. He is being. So it follows that he wants the beings he created in his own image to know who he *is*.

It also follows, then—considering we are made in the image of the Source of being—that we want to know who we are too. God is, and because he is, we also are, and if God wants to be known, it is logical that we, God's image-bearers, also want to be known. Underneath our search for ourselves, and even underneath the identity politics, assertions, and conflicts we see around us or engage in every day, something is happening that is very close to God's heart. It's just that we broken and wounded image bearers often get confused about the source of our identity. We think it's ourselves, our nationality, our political party, our denomination, our theology, our characteristics, or our preferences. But those are not where our core identity comes from.

Jesus is making himself vulnerable here in a spiritually charged location. These disciples are his closest friends. He loves them and he's been investing himself in them, but what if they still don't get what he's about? His biological brothers—Mary and Joseph's kids—don't get him. John the Baptizer almost didn't. So Jesus asks. And immediately, Peter exclaims, "I know, I know! You are the Messiah! God's promised anointed one! You are the Son of the one true God!"

Jesus is ecstatic. Yes! Someone understands! Jesus knows who he is, but now he also knows that what he's been saying and doing is getting through to somebody. What's more, Peter could not have come up with this on his own. None of the people in the crowds that the disciples quoted have said what Peter said. Which means somehow Jesus's beloved Father has communicated directly to Peter. "You got that from my Dad!" Jesus exclaims.

The whole situation is a win and a delight for Jesus. He feels known, and he now knows that he has made the Father known, and the Father has made him known. Peter is somehow in on the Father and Son's relationship. This is what Jesus came for—this kind of tight, interweaving relationship between us and him and the Father through the Holy Spirit—he prays insistently about it in John 17.

Because Peter has caught a glimpse of Jesus's true identity, he now gets a better look at his own. He gets a glimmer of insight into the new man he is becoming because of being with and focusing on Jesus. "Good for you, Simon son of Jonah!" Jesus cries out. "I'm calling you Peter—you're Rocky—and on this Rock I will build my church, so firmly that even Hades can't overcome it."

For much of history, and even in a notable branch or two of the Church today, people have taught that this story is about Jesus making Peter his successor as head of the Church—that is, the first Pope. At a glance, the interpretation makes sense. Jesus is punning in a glad but solemn way. (Who knew puns could be solemn?) "Rocky! I'm going to build my church on this Rock! *And* I'm giving you the keys of the Kingdom—authority to bind things up and set things free." How else would you interpret that?

Well, here's one way. Peter's name (*petros*), and the Rock (*petra*) on which Jesus plans to build his church, are not the same Greek word. Basically, "Peter," as we noticed in chapter 1, is a small stone or a pebble. "Petra" is like the enormous boulder on which the 200–year-old church I pastor was literally built. Jesus isn't saying Peter is the foundation of the church. That is not the identity Jesus is giving him. Jesus doesn't need a successor, because he himself is the foundation of the church, and (even though we haven't gotten to this part of the story yet) he is alive again, forever and ever. He's not going anywhere. He's immovable.

But there's a problem with the interpretation I just gave you. Often, "we're right, you're wrong" is as far as this teaching goes. We ignore the fact that, even if it's true that Jesus intended to pun and contrast two types of stone, he is still *making a pun* between Peter's name and that Rock foundation, and he does say some pretty surprising things about the authority that will be Peter's.

Looking into Peter's future (which we'll do in more detail in a few chapters), we discover he does become the physical human leader of the early church, right away at Pentecost. The Bible itself describes Peter's leadership. This is not just a legend in some church tradition somewhere. Peter is given notable authority. He continues to do miracles, and the words he speaks have power. But the Bible also demonstrates that he's fallible, and nothing here gives warrant to the succession of popes. So what do we do with this?

Here, I think, is what's happening in this passage. Jesus is noting Peter's transforming self in light of Peter's having perceived Jesus's own identity. When they first met, Jesus called Simon by the name Peter. And shortly after that, Peter called Jesus "Lord" and admitted he was a sinner. But now Peter's understanding of who Jesus is has gone to the next level. And so Peter's understanding of himself is also going to the next level. Peter's identity is derived directly from Jesus's identity.

Jesus is the Rock on which the church is built. But Peter is becoming like Jesus: teaching, healing, exorcising, and even walking on the water. And now he finds out that Jesus is even bestowing some of his own authority on him. Peter is like a stone chipped (or maybe even hewn) out of the giant foundation stone. He's smaller and you couldn't build a whole building on him, but he could be part of it. He's becoming a chip off the old block. All of this is identified in view of the disciples, and also presumably in view of the spiritual powers who are intent on doing all they can to overthrow both Jesus and the people getting close to him. Which may or may not have something to do with why, in the very next paragraph, Jesus's next name for Peter is so very much less flattering.

At least one of Jesus's disciples is starting to get a real picture of who Jesus truly is. Jesus has given that same disciple a little more insight about who he—the disciple—is becoming. Now it's time to start clueing the whole group of core disciples in, not only to what Jesus's identity is—Messiah, Son of the Living God—but to what that means.

Jesus hasn't talked about his suffering and death before. It is this conversation about Jesus's identity and Peter's identity that initiates Jesus's first revealing what's ahead for him. He spells it all out. Matthew says, "Jesus began to explain to his disciples that he must go to Jerusalem and suffer many things at the hands of the elders, the chief priests and the teachers of the law, and that he must be killed and on the third day be raised to life" (Matthew 16:21).

From our vantage point, we know this happened and also that none of the disciples understood any of it until after the fact.

But we might imagine that in the moment, this sounds a bit off to all of them. Especially to Peter, who has, after all, just been told he's a chip off the old "Rock," that God the Father himself has communicated something true to him about Jesus, and that the true thing is that Jesus is not only the promised Messiah, but also God's own Son. There is no good reason to imagine that suffering and death should be part of the experience of God's own Son. So Peter is indignant. What is Jesus's problem? Is he still depressed about his cousin? Still worn out from the crowds? What's the deal with this negative talk, especially when he was so happy and positive just two seconds ago?

With newfound confidence—seeing as Jesus has just told him he's getting the keys to the Kingdom—Peter takes Jesus aside and corrects him. "No, Lord!" he says. "That's not what's going to happen!" In context, I almost wonder whether Peter thinks he can prevent what Jesus said about suffering just by speaking against it. After all, Jesus has just told him he can bind and loose spiritual realities. But to his complete astonishment and dismay, his friend and Lord, who was just praising him for listening to the Father, turns on him . . . and calls him Satan? If Jesus disagreed, fair enough, but couldn't he have been a little more gentle? Instead, he lashes out at the one he couldn't say enough good about a moment ago.

Jesus does not have a personality disorder. This might sound unorthodox, but I don't think it's a stretch to say that Jesus got triggered. There is a reason he goes so far as to rebuke Satan here. Peter is presenting to Jesus precisely the same temptation that Satan presented to Jesus in the wilderness at the beginning of his ministry—to live an easier identity (Matthew 4:1–11,

Mark 1:12–13, Luke 4:1–13). Satan tried to get Jesus to take the easy route. To be a people-pleasing Messiah. To be a flashy-miracle Messiah. To be an expedient and successful Messiah. To follow his dreams, perhaps. Satan tried to get Jesus to "self-identify"—to define *himself* by his legitimate characteristics, instead of deriving his identity from his Father.

The temptation to identify ourselves self-referentially is how the serpent snagged Adam and Eve all the way back in the garden (Genesis 3). "If you eat this fruit, you will be like God," he told them. But they were already like God: made in God's image and given authority to reflect him, act on his behalf, and rule creation from his love. This is the human temptation—to "self-identify"—to define ourselves by ourselves, and leave God out of it entirely. When Peter says "This (suffering, torture, death) will never happen to you!" Jesus is triggered because he is actually tempted by this. That's why he says to Peter, "You are a stumbling block to me" (Matthew 16:23). Not a nice stone in the building, but one that can cause injury.

"Get behind me, Satan!" Jesus cries. In other words, "I recognize this trick. It's Satanic. You're holding me back, man. This completely defeats the reason I came here. You are presenting me with the easy way out all over again. I already resisted this in the desert. Don't bring it back, Satan."

Particularly given the Caesarea Philippi location of this interaction, I'm not sure Jesus was really even talking to Peter in that one exclamation. Maybe he really was talking to Satan, who was using a natural human response from Jesus's friend to make what sounded like a perfectly reasonable—and what's more, loyal—remark. The temptation didn't work when it came directly from Satan in the desert. But maybe the love between Jesus and his friend—a friend Jesus had just commended as hearing from his Father—could be leveraged instead.

Mercifully for Peter and all of us, Jesus recognizes the true author of the temptation and in his vehemence to shut it down, not to give in, he rebukes the tempter. *Then* he turns to Peter and says, in effect, "You heard from God the first time, but not this time—this is the way mere humans think." Well, he's right. This *is* the way humans think. We say things to each other that sound just like what Peter said, and we often hope to hear something like it from others when we're facing a difficult time: "You got this! Don't let those toxic people into your life. You deserve better. You need to take care of yourself."

Peter isn't saying anything beyond that, really. But in this case, Jesus calls it Satanic and then he starts talking about what it means to be a disciple. What it means is, apparently, to be like Jesus. In every way. I'm going to lay down my life, Jesus says. You need to lay down your life too, if you want to have any hope of discovering who you are. If you try to create your own identity, your life will slip right out of your hands.

Oh, Peter. Being like Jesus doesn't only mean you can heal the sick and feed the hungry and cast out demons (get behind me, Satan!) and preach about the Kingdom. It does mean that. It also means you get the keys to the Kingdom—and the keys are to take up your cross like Jesus, and give up your own life and will to Jesus. You know who Jesus is: the Messiah, the Son of the Living God! You just didn't know what it meant.

Jesus tells Peter, tells the Twelve, tells all of us, that for him to be the Christ, the Son of the Living God, it means he will give up the right to his self-identity. Philippians 2:6–8 tells us Jesus,

"Who, being in very nature God,
    did not consider equality with God something to
be used to his own advantage;
    [something to be grasped—hung onto]
rather, he made himself nothing
    by taking the very nature of a servant,
    being made in human likeness.
And being found in appearance as a man,
    he humbled himself
    by becoming obedient to death—
        even death on a cross!

Jesus sacrificed his true identity for us, taking on our sinful identity and dying for it. He tells us that for us to follow him, we have, somehow, to be like him in that. We have to do the same thing.

Satan tried to get even Jesus to self-identify with his legitimate characteristics: miracle worker, Son of God. Jesus knew that wasn't the way. Jesus "did not consider equality with God something to be used to his own advantage," but received his identity from his Father. He looks like his Father. God has always suffered over us. The only way for Jesus truly to reflect God, truly actively to be the Son of the living God, was to relinquish the right to his own identity and let his Father define him. Likewise, the only way to find out who we truly are is to let Jesus identify us, like he identified Peter, that chip off the old block.

On the other hand, Peter did not understand. He did not know why Jesus was triggered and had, seemingly, called him Satan. Neither he nor the other disciples understood that all this talk about the cross was literal. The Father had shown Peter that

Jesus was the Messiah, and that was enough for the moment. It would take some time for Jesus himself to communicate that his identity as the Messiah, the Son of the living God—and their own identities in connection with him—had to play out differently than Peter or the others anticipated.

In the meantime, Peter's own presuppositions were about to be reinforced.

FOLLOW MORE CLOSELY

Spend some time reflecting on the identity of Jesus. Who do you say that he is? What does that mean? Create a doodle, a drawing, a collage depicting the name you associate with Jesus or the meaning behind it.

CHAPTER 5

MOUNTAIN-TOP EXPERIENCE

Matthew 17:1–9; Mark 9:1–10; Luke 9:28–36

teach a class through The Pilgrimage, the online spiritual formation community I direct, called *Stepping Into the Story*. During one of the twelve weeks of this life-mapping course, we focus on epiphanies. We talk about how epiphanies are moments when we are surprised by clarity or a whole new perspective, but we also note that the clarity and new perspective don't usually initiate any major life change right away. Often they are simply the first step, setting us up for new directions or ways of life that we will need to adopt later. In between the epiphany and what we might call a conversion—that is, a substantive change of life— there are a whole lot of our old assumptions still in play, which, in spite of the epiphany we had, we're not yet aware of.

For example, in approximately 2006, I had a lightbulb moment that I can only assume came from the Holy Spirit— considering I was content in my complementarian[12] views at the time—that women are free to lead and preach and teach in the Christian church. It was very startling and very clear . . . but I still didn't particularly *like* the idea of women preachers, and I certainly didn't think I was ever going to be one myself. I assumed the epiphany was simply to help me be a better friend and support to women who did feel called to the pastorate. I hadn't been a very good one up to this point. Eventually I did go back to seminary, more open to the idea of the pastorate myself, but it took another dozen years or so before I actually became the pastor of a church, and even then, I hadn't been looking. I was contentedly engaged in directing The Pilgrimage and working as a hospice chaplain. This is what I mean about the lag time between epiphany and transformation.

Peter and two of the other disciples are about to have an epiphany. This epiphany is even more striking than mine, but neither Peter, James, nor John are even permitted, let alone inclined, to do anything with it right away. And it's debatable whether the blinding light of clarity in fact managed to clarify anything for Peter at all. If we were going to debate this, I would argue that it didn't.

A week or two ago in Caesarea Philippi, Jesus asked the disciples who they said he was, and Peter enthusiastically answered with the reality of his growing impression: "You're the Messiah, the Son of the living God!" Jesus agreed with him and even told him that Jesus's own Father, God, had communicated that to Peter somehow. But then Jesus started saying all kinds of crazy stuff about torture and dying. It didn't match up with "Messiah, Son of the living God." At all. So Peter tried to redirect Jesus's self-destructive train of thought, and Jesus lashed out and called him Satan. That was unsettling, and Peter didn't even get a chance to recover from the emotional whiplash, because Jesus just turned around again and invited him, James, and John on a hike.

The invitation is surely related to what just happened, considering all three Gospel writers who tell this story maintain the same order of events here. Which means it must have been an awkward hike. What do those guys talk about? Does Peter feel like he's being taken on a really long walk to the woodshed? Also, why are James and John there? True, they were originally Peter's business partners, but Andrew was part of that group, so why isn't he coming along? Besides, this isn't a fishing trip. We're frequently told that these three were Jesus's closest friends, although the only other story in which we see all three of them selected apart from the other disciples until the Garden of Gethsemane is a story where Jesus raises a little girl from the dead (Matthew 9:18–26; Mark 5:21–43; Luke 8:40–56).

On the other hand, maybe the choice of which disciples to take on this hike really was that simple—that they were Jesus's three closest friends. Jesus did give James and John a nickname too: "Sons of Thunder" (Mark 3:17). They had to share it, though, so when he wrote his Gospel much, much later, John gave himself a new one—"the disciple Jesus loved" (John 13:23). James and John demonstrated their chutzpah—but also their sense of closeness to Jesus—by later vying for position as Jesus's right- and left-hand men (Matthew 20:20–28; Mark 10:35–37).

Maybe Jesus chose these three not simply because they were his closest friends, but because all three of them understood in a way the others didn't that he was really the Messiah. All three of them also had some mistaken impressions about what that meant. Maybe he chose them precisely because he knew each one was interested in being second in command when the Kingdom as they understood it arrived, and he wanted to give them a reality check. Maybe he was aware of the rivalry among the three, which the Gospel writers hint at, and maybe he wanted to tone it down before the suffering and death he had begun to predict finally occurred.

To be honest, we don't know what Jesus is thinking as he leads his three friends away from the others in Caesarea Philippi, and Peter maybe doesn't have any better idea than we do. He's probably feeling a little apprehensive. Is he about to have his impressions about Jesus as the Messiah, the Son of the living God, confirmed before this pair of brothers—his partners and rivals—or is he about to be shamed before them even further?

Strangely, neither Matthew, Mark, nor Luke tell us which mountain Jesus and his friends hiked. Maybe they thought we should be able to guess. In that case, though, they probably should have given us more clues, because there are two traditional options—Mount Tabor and Mount Hermon—and to be honest, I'm skeptical about both of them. The Gospel writers don't even all agree on exactly how long it took Jesus, Peter, James, and John to get there. They record a range of six to eight days to get to and hike up this unnamed mountain. Possibly for that reason, tradition (and a Franciscan church still standing on the spot) tells us that this mountain was Mount Tabor. The problem with Tabor as a location is that other than the event we're about to look at right now, the First Testament events surrounding this mountain[13] don't seem overly relevant to what happens in today's story. Evidently the Emperor Constantine's mother, Queen Helena, was the one who selected Tabor as the site of the Transfiguration and everyone just went with it.[14] Who knows? Maybe she was right.

More recent teaching favors Mount Hermon, which is in Caesarea Philippi, where Jesus and the disciples were when Peter was identifying Jesus as the Messiah, the Son of the living God, and assuring him he would not suffer and be killed. In my opinion, Mount Hermon is a much more plausible location because unlike Tabor, it does have a specific significance.

Even before Jesus's day, when Mount Hermon was believed by pagans to be Pan's grotto,[15] it had dark spiritual associations. Michael S. Heiser notes that some Hebrew traditions selected this location as the spot where the rebelling angels were cast out of heaven. Heiser declares, "Bashan [the Hebrew name for Caesarea Philippi] and Hermon were ground zero for the cosmic evil powers."[16] He then says, "In a few days, Jesus would take three disciples with Him up into Mount Hermon and put the entire spiritual world on notice with the Transfiguration."[17] The idea is compelling, but if Heiser and others are right, then why did Jesus take a week or more to bring his friends up there for this momentous event, if they were already there? Isn't that a bit anticlimactic?

It seems likely that "putting the spiritual world on notice" in that specific, notable location was what Jesus had already done when he asked his disciples who they believed him to be, when he affirmed Peter's declaration that Jesus was the Messiah, the Son of the living God, when he declared he would build his church on "this rock" and that the gates of the underworld would not prevail, and when he began to discuss how all this was going to happen—through his suffering and death. I want to argue that, while still retaining cosmic significance, what Peter, James, and John were about to witness on the top of this unnamed mountain was intended to be more of a statement to them than to the evil spiritual powers, to prepare them and fortify them for what was going to happen next.

Which is why, despite the scholars and traditions overwhelmingly favoring other locations, I am nevertheless arguing for a third location. Because the Transfiguration seems to be more for the benefit of Jesus himself and the three friends he brought with him, I'm inclined to doubt either of the usually-designated locations for the event. I suspect the stated travel time of approximately a week is a lowball estimate indicating that some vague time elapsed. The number of days may even be symbolic.

Seven is the biblical number designating perfection or completeness, and since both six and eight are numbers on either side of it, they may at minimum signify that something momentous, but not fully realized, is about to happen. Further, according to some sources, in Jewish numerology the number six symbolizes the physical created world and the number eight symbolizes the covenant with God.[18] The event Jesus's disciples are about to witness draws on both realities. My very strong impression, for the reasons we have already discussed, and for a few more we'll look at in a minute, is that Jesus led his friends to Mount Sinai. (For the record, nobody is really sure where Mount Sinai is either, and the quickest someone could walk to the closest theorized mountain from Caesarea Philippi is about eleven days.[19])

By now you may be wishing you could ask me why location—Sinai or anywhere else—even matters. It matters because while they're hanging out up there, all of a sudden Peter's earlier declaration that Jesus is in fact the Messiah, the one promised

to the Hebrew people from ages past, gets confirmed in a very
Hebrew, covenant-specific way. Jesus is transformed before the
disciples' eyes, and two deeply significant forerunners of this
Messiah—both of whom have a history with Mount Sinai—
show up. These two newcomer-but-old-timers are Moses, who
received the Law of God on Mount Sinai, and Elijah the prophet,
who confronted God and was recommissioned to God's service
on Mount Sinai.

If Mount Sinai could be our location, it's also easier to
understand how Peter, James, and John could have known
who these two mysterious presences, showing up "in glorious
splendor" (Luke 9:30) were. It's not like there was photographic
evidence of what they looked like, and in any case, it would have
been against the very law these two upheld to have made images
of them (Exodus 20:4–6). We also don't get the impression that
Jesus introduced them—all three Gospel accounts of this story
just tell us that Moses and Elijah show up and Jesus talks with
them, almost as if he forgets his other three friends are even there.
When the Father speaks, he introduces Jesus, not the visitors.
Do Moses and Elijah have props to identify themselves? Some
stone tablets and a fiery chariot, maybe? Or, as I suspect, do Peter
and the other two know immediately who these men are because
of *where* they are? Only two men in the Hebrew Scriptures had
identity-defining, direction-changing epiphanies on a mountain,
and in both of those cases, the mountain was Sinai.

Now here are three ordinary fisher-guys having an epiphany
on this same mountain, and it is epic. We might call it "Old
Testament level." Their rabbi is glowing so brightly they can
barely look at him. He's talking, in person, right in front of them,
with Moses who represents the Law of God, and Elijah who

represents the Prophets.[20] Between the two of them, they stand in for two of the three major sections of the Hebrew Scriptures, all of which set the stage for the Messiah. Also between the two of them is the Word of God made flesh-and-glowing—and who could plausibly stand in for the third section, the Writings. The Writings include literature—wisdom through poetry and story. Life with Jesus yields both.

Maybe Peter, James, and John don't discern all this symbolism and significance right off the bat. On the other hand, among the Jewish people of Jesus's day, even fishermen would most likely have had a pretty good working knowledge of their Scriptures. It's entirely possible that John, for example, who much later wrote that "the Word became flesh and made his dwelling among us" (John 1:14), picked up the first intimations of that idea during this event. But in the moment, it's Peter who does the talking.

Things are a little hazy. Peter can't exactly articulate the significance of what he is seeing, but he knows who Moses and Elijah are, and evidently his rabbi knows them personally. Somehow these three are connected and from all appearances, God is getting the band back together. Then it gets literally hazy—a cloud descends over everybody—so it's hard to see anything at all. It's so hazy, all three Gospel writers who tell us this story give different versions of why Peter responds the way he does. Matthew just lets Peter be responsible for his own outburst. Mark says Peter, James, and John were really frightened and Peter, clearly feeling the need to say something—and perhaps remind Jesus that they're still there too—just blurts out, "Hey! This is amazing—and what a great venue! Let's make you guys some cabins. We can sell tickets . . ." Luke doesn't say they were frightened, but sleepy.

It seems like all the things could be true—if Jesus and his buddies had been hiking for days, they were probably all tired, and even though I've always pictured this event happening in broad daylight, there's nothing in the texts that explicitly tells us this, except for the haze itself. Perhaps it was early morning—Jesus had a habit of getting up before everyone else to talk to his Father. Maybe he had been doing just that, and as the disciples wake up and start shuffling around getting breakfast, Jesus's two friends from ages past arrive, right back at the spot where they had met him before, and Jesus starts shining like a lighthouse. The whole event would have been alarming regardless, but if you were still groggy from sleep and then some ancient saints showed up out of nowhere while your best friend spontaneously lit up like a torch, it would be even more frightening and disorienting. I mean, I would probably start babbling too.

On the other hand, even if Peter didn't understand the full implications of what he was suggesting, he must have meant something of what he said. Maybe that is why Matthew doesn't give him any convenient excuses for saying it. A week (or two) ago, Peter declared that Jesus was the Messiah, the Son of the living God. In return, Jesus told him that God his Father had revealed that to Peter directly. Then Jesus said some depressing stuff about suffering and dying. But then they took this long hike to and up this very high mountain. Now here are two of the most pivotal figures in Hebrew history—one of whom died but was buried only God knew where (Deuteronomy 34:5–7) and the other of whom hadn't even died but was transported into the heavens in a fiery chariot with horses (2 Kings 2:11–12).

And so maybe, Peter imagines, Jesus has been speaking in parables again—all that stuff about suffering and dying. Maybe death is different for spiritual giants like this. But maybe also the Messiah was going to be a different sort of leader than he had at first thought. Moses and Elijah were more spiritual warriors than physical ones. So far Jesus hadn't gotten particularly warlike about anything, but he did have an outsized amount of divine wisdom.

These three could live in the shrines Peter, James, and John would build them. Then the three disciples could serve the three saints. Surely this is why the three of them had been selected to accompany Jesus on this very special trip. At a minimum, the disciples could be their errand boys, and that would be enough of an honor. But more than likely they are being chosen to be lead officers in the Messiah's militia, right? This mountain would be basecamp, where the three dignitaries would strategize, and Peter, James, and John would carry out their orders.

Before Peter can get too carried away, though—or even really finish his thought—a thick cloud descends over everyone, muffling his words so they can hear another voice. This is the voice of the one who had already communicated to Peter that Jesus was the Messiah and God's Son. "This is my Son," says the voice, audibly this time, "whom I love; with him I am well pleased. Listen to him!" (Matthew 17:5).

Listen to him.

Was this an affirmation of Peter's first, second, third impressions? Was it a correction? Was God, Jesus's own Father, warning Peter and his friends not to get ahead of themselves? Was the whole encounter the Father's reframe—or even replay— of the identity-revealing scene that had happened between Jesus and Peter a week or two before?

Jesus himself had also experienced emotional whiplash that day. His good friend Peter had expressed both the truth of Jesus's identity from his Father and the temptation of his Adversary, in what must almost have felt like one breath. Jesus had begun to face the horror of suffering and death that was coming and had started to try to express some of it to his friends and followers. But instead of supporting him in it, Peter had tried to talk him out of it. Jesus needed to get grounded if he was going to move forward. He needed to hear directly from his Father who he was so he could be that person. And he needed at least a couple of people—at least the friends with whom he felt closest—to hear it, to see it too. He needed to be seen and known for who he really was.

Once again, Peter assumed he knew what "Messiah, Son of the living God" meant. Once again he had spoken up with a well-intentioned good idea—"Let's set up a base camp here for you all!" Once again, the Father confirmed—this time out loud for the others to hear—that Peter was right. Jesus was his own Son. What's more, he was delighted in that Son. But also, and because of that, this Son of his needed to be listened to. Heard. Not contradicted.

The voice of the Father cut through the haze, but when the cloud lifted, Moses and Elijah were gone. Jesus just looked like himself—the guy these three disciples knew and loved and trusted. The guy who had called the three of them away from their boats to fish for people. And now they knew him on a deeper level. They knew him in a different way from the other men and women who followed Jesus around. They had seen him glowing. They had seen him talking familiarly with heroes of old. There had been something entirely surreal about the whole event, but all three of them had witnessed the same thing, so they couldn't ever imagine they had just made it up.

And now they are heading down the mountain, and Jesus is speaking to them, and they are listening. "Don't tell anyone about this," Jesus says. "Not until the Son of Man has risen from the dead." *Son of Man* was Jesus's nickname for himself. It's intriguing that he referred to himself that way immediately after God his Father had spoken up for him as Son of God.

But maybe that was the point. The Father had publicly claimed Jesus as his own, to Jesus's closest friends on earth. Now on the strength of that, Jesus could face the enormous, momentous thing that he had come to do—which was identify so closely with humanity that he would take full responsibility for its rebellion against his Father whom he loved, who loved him, who was pleased with him.

Now he could talk to these friends about rising from the dead. Death had to come first. Nobody could fully know who he was until then. But death would not be the end, and one day Peter—and James and John too—would be able to tell the rest of the group what they had seen that day. Rising from the dead sounds a lot more hopeful than torture and death, and anyway, Peter and his buddies were listening to Jesus, like the Father commanded them. They mused together about what "rising from the dead" could mean, as Mark tells us (Mark 9:10). But apparently Jesus didn't enlighten them.

And honestly, it doesn't seem like in the moment the whole epiphany did much to enlighten them, either. Maybe that was the main reason Jesus told Peter and the brothers to keep the experience quiet until they saw how it was going to play out.

He had heard Peter's "shelters" idea even though the Father had interrupted him. He knew if these guys said a thing about it, they were going to misrepresent everything because they still didn't get it. Maybe the transfiguration was really more for Jesus's own benefit, even though it was important to him that these three friends bear witness to it. Or maybe, like the epiphanies we have in our own lives, these three—who were going to end up being leaders in Jesus's new community—needed to see something mind-blowing, even if they didn't understand it right away, so their minds could open to receive what was coming next.

FOLLOW MORE CLOSELY

Have you ever had an epiphany that felt like it came from God? What was it? How do you interpret it? Has it changed anything about you or the direction of your life? If so, how? If not, what do you predict about its impact?

CHAPTER 6

LET DOWN

John 13:1–17, 31–38; Matthew 26:69–75

piritual highs come and go, and when they go, they really go. There have been three times in my life where I have lived through a spiritual experience that was so powerful and wonderful that the next day, I felt like I was recovering from a long, serious illness. For example, the day after my ordination in 2019, the most physical movement I could manage and the most mental activity I could handle was to sit in my home office and put used postage stamps in my stamp collection album from middle school. And then, to be honest, for the rest of that week, I had a very hard time remembering that what had happened that day was God's doing, not mine. It was for God's purposes, and not really about me or even about the congregation I had been called to shepherd. I started getting sidetracked. "How do I live up to this?" I thought.

I forgot that while God and the congregation gave me a new part of my identity that day (Pastor—Reverend, even), the pressure was not on me to define what that means. I simply need to remain open to God's helping me to live what he has made me to be and do for the time God intends me to be and do it. But it's not that surprising that I hit a low right after the high. There's documented evidence, both in Scripture and in church history, that this kind of thing happens to God's people a lot. It happened to Peter.

As we've journeyed with Peter, we've seen Jesus challenge his expectations time and again. Each time Peter rises to the challenge and is transformed a little more. Recently, Jesus has begun to try to upend yet another of Peter's expectations for how the world works. This time, though, the expectation isn't really shifting. The episode hasn't resolved. The assumption is too ingrained to be overturned so easily—even by the voice of God from the heavens, apparently.

Part of Peter's expectation was, I imagine, that it was his job to name, or to identify, the self. In the hyper-individualistic culture in which I—and quite possibly you—live, we want to self-name or self-identify. Peter's culture would have been more communal and interdependent. So maybe his expectation was that the family or community determines a person's identity. This, along with Jesus's verbally granting him the keys of the Kingdom, probably explains why he was so comfortable naming Jesus as "Messiah, the Son of the living God," and why he felt so certain he knew what that meant. And honestly, even in a hyper-individualistic society, we can become super invested in our own perceptions of who another person is. Or maybe someone has done that to us. Regardless of social context then, typically the naming or identifying of self or others is humanly determined. Naming happens in a human-enclosed loop.

In fact, we are hard-wired to name things. The first task that God gave the first human in the garden of Eden was to name the animals (Genesis 2:19–20). But naming in the Bible (and in some cultures even still) often implies control, or a type of ownership. When that first as-yet sinless human named the animals, the person was exercising the appropriate creation authority that God had granted. God intended for humans to represent his loving and ordering care and authority over the rest of creation. It's possible that this early-human act of naming was a calling out and observation of the characteristics God had put into each animal, and also an assigning of the animal's identity. But even before humans rebelled against God and corrupted our authority, God did not intend us to assign identity to each other—or even ourselves—in that same authoritative way. We were to have authority over creation, while God would have authority over us. Therefore, God is the one who determines a human's identity— not just our true names, but what those names mean.

Jesus spoke into the expectation of self- (or community-) determination. Peter had named him correctly: the Messiah, the Son of the living God. But neither Peter nor anyone else had the authority to define what that name or identity meant. Peter assumed, as surely any of us would have, that "Messiah"— especially "Son of the living God"—meant sweet success from now on. To his consternation, Jesus informed him, "It means I'm going to suffer and die. It means I lay aside my rights. I lay down who you want me to be and who I might prefer to be. And if you want to keep being transformed into someone like me, you're going to have to do the same thing."

We humans are great at not understanding, or not hearing, or misinterpreting things we don't like the sound of. We don't want to face hard or scary truths, and if it scares us enough, we do whatever it takes to convince ourselves that the meaning of something isn't the true meaning at all. For once, Jesus wasn't speaking in parables. There was nothing metaphorical about his impending suffering and death. But his disciples needed a way to manage their fears, so rather than asking Jesus about it, they just decided he didn't mean what he was saying. They didn't understand, partly because their idea of Messiah didn't include the possibility of his suffering and death, but mostly because they didn't want to. They found ways to prove that their own understanding was right.

Besides, by now Peter, James, and John have seen Jesus transfigured before their eyes in glorified form. They got to see a glowing Jesus hanging out with Moses and Elijah. Even though Peter's idea to set up a basecamp on the mountaintop for the three dignitaries got shot down—or, let's be honest, totally ignored—he took the epiphany as yet another sign that yes! Jesus is the Messiah, Son of living God, which means triumphant, obviously, because Jesus said that stuff about rising from the dead. If Peter was already thinking that the Messiah's death was metaphorical—maybe it just meant they were going to go through hard times, which was of course to be expected—it's not hard to imagine "rising from the dead" as metaphorical too. Something like, "Things are going to get tough for a while, but then we will triumph!" Besides, Peter and James and John had discussed the meaning of "rising from the dead" in front of Jesus, and he hadn't corrected them. "Triumphant" must be who Jesus really is! And because Peter was so invested in maintaining that image of the Messiah, the Son of the Living God, his own transformation got stuck.

Something Peter may not have known, and which is all too easy to forget even if you do know it, is that whole-person transformation takes time. Always. In the process, often our expectations for how the world works creep back in and begin to take over our expectations of Jesus. We're about to jump from the clear-but-unclear epiphany that was Jesus's transfiguration, all the way forward to his washing his disciples' feet. And we'll discover that in all that time, Peter's way of relating to Jesus has not progressed at all.

Both when Peter named Jesus as the Messiah and God's Son, as well as in this foot-washing interaction, we see that Jesus knows who he is. He demonstrates his divinity and authority through servanthood. When he acknowledged his status as the Messiah, Son of the living God, he immediately began talking about laying down his life. Even at the time of his transfiguration, when he told Peter, James, and John about rising from the dead, the implication was that, well, he was going to die. This time he doesn't just tell but shows this identity.

> Jesus knew that the Father had put all things under his power, and that he had come from God and was returning to God; so he got up from the meal took off his outer clothing, and wrapped a towel around his waist . . . and began to wash his disciples' feet . . . (John 13:3–5).

Did you catch that? *Because* Jesus knew who he was and where (or who!) he came from—because he had power directly from the Father over literally everything—he was able to serve. Jesus's humility and servanthood came from absolute security in who he was in God, not from a sense of obligation, codependence, passive aggression, or self-hatred, which may underlie many of our reasons for serving. He served his disciples freely because he loved them and knew who he was.

In both the previous story and this one, Peter identifies Jesus correctly and enthusiastically. He has already named Jesus as the Messiah and God's Son. Today he calls him Lord. But unlike Jesus, he still misunderstands what Jesus's messiahship and lordship mean. Once again, he has taken his eyes off Jesus and is putting his faith in how he understands the world to work. A lord "lords it over" people. Someone with authority bosses people around. Expects to be served. Gets angry for no reason. But also, a lord can give his buddies a hand up if he wants to. Once again, Jesus flips over Peter's expectations. And this time, Peter doesn't understand any better than he did maybe a year ago.

In fact, he loses it just like he did before. "No way, Lord!" he says. "You're the *Master*. Don't wash my feet!" Hear the echoes: "Never, Lord! This will never happen to you!" Just like before, Jesus tries to set Peter straight. "I can only be your Lord if you let me serve you. If I am your Lord, you need to follow my example and serve too." Even though the cross is closer than ever, Jesus uses the language of servanthood and not death here. Still, his response is essentially the same: I fulfill who I am by laying down my rights, so that you can become who you are too.

Peter's reaction—"Well, in that case, just give me a bath, Jesus!"—shows that he's still missing the point. We can tell, though, that he is deeply touched. Besides, we already know his love for Jesus is real. So when Jesus says, "I've gotta leave, you guys, and this time you can't come with me," Peter wants to go too! "What do you mean I can't go with you? I love you! I'd die for you!"

Peter just wants—has always wanted, since Jesus made him into a fisher of men—to be where Jesus is all the time. And maybe he doesn't really think that Jesus will be killed, but he has to admit that Jesus has been saying that thing about laying down your life, and Peter has already dedicated his whole life to the guy. He's given up his livelihood so it's not a stretch to throw in the promise to lay down his life for Jesus too. "See? I've been listening to you. This is what you said to do. I'm willing to do it!" But Jesus calls him out—probably a little sadly. "No, Peter, you won't. Instead, by the time the rooster's waking everyone up, you will have disowned me three times already."

After that, Jesus and the disciples head to the Garden of Gethsemane. Jesus is arrested, and he just lets the soldiers take him. Peter makes an attempt to defend Jesus by cutting off a guy's ear. He's willing to lay down his life—but only after putting up a fight. That's how the world works, right? Even laying down your life for someone means you go down swinging. You do that on behalf of the person you're willing to die for. But cutting off Malchus's ear doesn't help. Jesus just puts it back on again, and rebukes Peter once more. Then almost everybody runs away as Jesus is hauled off to an illegal trial in the dark.

Peter doesn't run away, though, and John doesn't run away. Peter has told Jesus he will die for him, and John has connections, so they go to the high priest's house where this mock trial is being held, to see what can be done there. When they arrive, John can get inside, but Peter has to wait in the courtyard with the high priest's servants and other random people.

Even though there are people nearby, spiritually speaking, Peter is alone. After three years of following a miraculous rabbi with a band of brothers and sisters, he is suddenly completely on his own. He doesn't know these other people. His buddy and friendly rival John has managed to get inside to be near Jesus. But Peter, the activist, is now pretty much useless, and the person he loves more than anyone in the world is in trouble and Peter can't get to him. None of this was supposed to happen. God, Jesus's real Father, had told Peter—twice!—that Jesus was God's Son. Ever since then, Peter has been trying his hardest to convince Jesus of this—that the Messiah can't be arrested and tortured and killed. But now Jesus *is* arrested, and things are becoming horrible, and Jesus's Father isn't stepping in, and what if the world still works exactly the way Peter always knew it did? Peter is afraid.

Here is what I always—literally always until I prepared this study for the first time—used to think was Peter's problem in this story: I thought he was afraid of being killed. Maybe fear of an untimely death was part of it, but here's the thing—Peter had already told Jesus he was willing to die for him. He already physically tried to defend Jesus. And unlike everyone else except John, he did not run away when Jesus was captured, but followed Jesus as far as he was able to go. That being true, it seems unlikely that all of a sudden he chickened out. If he had chickened out, he probably would only have had the opportunity to disown Jesus once. If he were that afraid of dying, he would've peeled out of there after the first servant girl called him out as a follower. He didn't. He stuck around. But he was afraid.

I believe Peter was afraid with the kind of fear that makes you angry. You know that kind, right? Parents feel it when their children put themselves in harm's way—after you find out your kid is okay, often you yell at them. We see angry-fear in social media at all ends of the sociopolitical spectrum—if the wrong person gets into the wrong office, the world is going to end, and until that happens, we're all going to yell at each other about how monstrous the opposite side is. (To be fair, there is a lot of monstrosity out there.) Peter is hanging out in the courtyard of a high priest, where he's probably never been before, and this servant girl realizes he's not from the household, but she recognizes him, so she says, "Oh—you're one of that Galilee-Jesus's followers." And Peter, because he is afraid enough to be angry, snaps, in the hearing of the whole crowd around the fire, "What are you even talking about?"

That's awkward. He doesn't leave, but he does move away from the fire, into the gateway. There are people there too, but evidently not the same crowd. Maybe he can blend in here. Another serving girl walks by, notices him despite his best efforts, says, "Hey, aren't you one of those guys who follow Jesus around?" And Peter's so angry-frightened, he denies it with an oath (the kind of thing Jesus told us not to do in the Sermon on the Mount (Matthew 5:33–37).

Finally, someone gets up the nerve to approach this belligerent northerner a third time. "But . . . but you have to be one of his followers. You have the accent." Now Peter is so terrified, he is utterly furious. Matthew tells us he starts all-out cursing. "I. Don't. Know. The man!" And suddenly, the rooster crows. So, what was Peter afraid of?

I think he was afraid he was telling the truth.

I don't really believe Peter was self-reflective enough to have said to Jesus right then, "I don't even know who you are anymore!" But I wonder if the fear that was quietly sneaking in at the back of his mind said that maybe, after three amazing years, he really didn't know Jesus at all. He had seen and done amazing things while following this rabbi, this soul craftsman, and he had thought the whole world was changed. Impossible numbers of fish could be caught, sick bodies healed, captive spirits freed. Uncountable people could be fed. Water could be walked on like dry ground. And there was a Kingdom coming, one they had all been preaching about since they hit the road three years ago. Peter thought Jesus was the King of it. Jesus himself admitted that he was the Messiah, the Son of the living God, when Peter confessed it. The Father audibly claimed Jesus as his Son and Peter saw two notable figures from Scripture to confirm that Jesus was the embodied fulfillment of all that Scripture promised.

But in light of all that, Peter had become so convinced that nothing bad could happen to someone like Jesus. Even though Jesus had been warning him and the others about it for ages now, Peter still hadn't understood it or accepted it. Now, here in the high priest's courtyard, it looks like everything he ever thought about this man was just too good to be true. Suddenly Jesus is arrested. He's being interrogated by religious leaders in a trial held in secret, in a private home, at midnight, which goes against the tenets those very religious leaders preach. They are corrupt, and it looks like they are winning, and maybe the world really only does work the way Peter thought it did all along, back when he was just Simon, the responsible fisherman.

Peter doesn't know it, but spiritually and metaphorically, he has stepped out of the boat again to get to Jesus—following him to the garden, cutting off Malchus's ear, getting all the way to the home of the high priest. But now that he's there, Jesus is nowhere to be seen. Only the wind and the waves. Only the darkness and chaos of the world, behaving exactly as Peter had been so convinced it never would—never could—again. He is sinking, and there is no one to cry out to. And so, in his terror and doubt, he lashes out at the one he loves the most, swearing up and down that he never knew him.

Back in the 1500s in Spain, there was a monk who is now known as San Juan de la Cruz (Saint John of the Cross), who did a lot of thinking and writing about the human soul, in particular a phenomenon that he called the "dark night of the soul." I believe that here in the high priest's courtyard, Peter is having one.

Usually a dark night of the soul lasts much longer than Peter's does. But like a person experiencing such a thing, he is going through a time during which everything he thinks he knows about God—or specifically about Jesus—is thrown out of certainty. A dark night of the soul is often triggered by an upsetting or even traumatic event, but it isn't the event itself. The dark night is a sense you have that in the middle of that difficult event or season, that God has abandoned you. That God really isn't who you thought he was, and you are all alone. A person in the middle of a dark night of the soul may be depressed, but the depression isn't the dark night either. The darkness is all about the relationship with God. The relationship itself feels dark. There is a lack of clarity. You may want to pray but find praying impossible. You may want to read the Bible but not be able to understand a word. Sometimes people going through a dark night feel like they're losing their faith. It's scary, and quite often a person going through it is scared enough to get angry—maybe even at God.

Even though the dark night of the soul is scary, it can be a gift from God, who intends it to move our relationship with him to a deeper, more intimate, more mature, more transformed level. It's a crucible. It shows what our faith is really made of, and it burns out impurities. Whether the experience does all these things has, perhaps, more to do with a persons' choice in the darkness to continue to reach out for God—even if it means reaching out to figuratively beat on God's chest—or to turn in on themselves and leave God out of the picture entirely. I believe there was another person going through a similar experience at just about the time Peter was. I think it was Judas. Peter wasn't, after all, the only one who had his expectations disappointed by Jesus.

Judas also thought Jesus was going to take over the world, and he didn't understand any better than Peter did what Jesus meant about suffering and dying and losing one's life to find it. It also seems likely that he never understood even as much as Peter did about who Jesus was. He certainly didn't have the same experiences that Peter had. I am not sure whether Judas ever truly realized or accepted the idea that Jesus was the Son of the living God. Maybe he thought he could force Jesus's hand to be the Messiah they all wanted. But Jesus wouldn't be forced to self-identify and assert his own rights—not by Peter ("No, Lord! This will never happen to you!") nor by Judas, who may have set up the arrest in hopes that Jesus would finally show his power.

We know how Judas responded to his disappointment in Jesus. He realized he had sentenced an innocent man—but also an innocent man who apparently didn't have the power Judas thought he had—and Judas despaired and took his own life. But what about Peter? He had declared and believed that Jesus was the Messiah, the Son of the Living God. Even if he didn't understand exactly what that meant, he had known it to be true. So what kind of metal would the crucible of the dark night of the soul show him to be? Would he shatter like Judas, or would he, as Job said—who went through a prolonged dark night himself— "come forth as gold" (Job 23:10).

Maybe Peter didn't know who Jesus was anymore, but Jesus still knew Peter. He had called out the denial before it even happened. Luke tells us that at the moment of the last denial, at the moment of the rooster's crow, Jesus came out from the false trial and caught Peter's eye (Luke 22:60–61). And that, not the fear of getting caught, was what made Peter finally run out of the garden, as the Gospels say, weeping bitterly.

When I've read this story before, I always imagined that when Peter said he would die for Jesus, and Jesus told him he would deny him instead, the conversation went something like this:

Peter: I'll go with you! I'd die for you!

Jesus: No you won't, you wuss. By the time the rooster crows this morning, you'll have told everybody three times you never even heard of me.

Like a rebuke before the fact. But I don't think that anymore. Now I think Jesus was holding out a glimmer of hope to Peter. "No friend, you won't die for me," he's saying. "It's going to get dark here for a while, and you're going to end up thinking—and saying—you don't know me. But you know from experience it's darkest before the dawn, and when the rooster crows, you'll know the light is coming."

I doubt Peter understood that in the moment. When Jesus looked at him after the last denial, I imagine Peter's emotions were all tangled up and he couldn't bear the gaze. He had fulfilled his Lord's prediction. He had said he didn't know Jesus—three times. He meant to die for him, and he had disowned him instead. He had let Jesus down. And I imagine too, that for Peter, the dark night of the soul wasn't quite over yet. He knew he had let Jesus down, but he couldn't help feeling that Jesus had let him down too, and he just didn't know what to do with those feelings. He was so ashamed, and so disappointed, that he rushed out of the courtyard, weeping bitterly.

FOLLOW MORE CLOSELY

Lectio divina is an ancient way of reading the Bible. We did something like it in chapter 2. This time we'll read a portion of Psalm 30. The first time you read it, simply read for content. What is the psalmist saying? On the second read-through, let the words sink in deeper. What kinds of emotions are being expressed? Can you imagine Peter praying something like this? Can you imagine yourself praying it? The third time you read, try really praying it. What experience, dynamic, or concern do you find yourself connecting with these words? Pray it a few times if it feels especially relatable. Then spend some time sitting in silence, leaving that prayer there between you and God. Does God say anything back?

Psalm 30:5–10

Weeping may stay for the night,
but rejoicing comes in the morning.
When I felt secure, I said,
"I will never be shaken."
LORD, when you favored me,
you made my royal mountain stand firm;
but when you hid your face,

I was dismayed.
To you, Lord, I called;
to the Lord I cried for mercy:
"What is gained if I am silenced,
if I go down to the pit?
Will the dust praise you?
Will it proclaim your faithfulness?
Hear, Lord, and be merciful to me;
Lord, be my help."

CHAPTER 7

A NEW JOB ALL OVER AGAIN

John 20:1–10, 21

We don't know where Peter went after he rushed out of the courtyard weeping bitterly with a rooster crowing in the background. He might have been at the crucifixion, I suppose, but the only one of the original twelve men who is mentioned in the Gospels as being there is John, with the women disciples. Besides, as we've noted, Peter was a bit conflicted in his relationship with Jesus at the time. Both his shame at having disowned Jesus three times and his disappointment in Jesus's not living up to his expectations might have made the already horrific spectacle of the crucifixion even harder to face, so it's entirely possible that in his fear and sorrow, he went off somewhere by himself while all that was happening.

He would have wanted to sort himself out. He had become almost accustomed to Jesus's surprising him by now, but this was the worst, most disappointing surprise he ever could have *not* imagined. A dark night of the soul is scary because it is disorienting. It feels like abandonment by God and loss of faith. It feels something like dying. If you're building your identity around Jesus the Messiah, as Peter was, and suddenly Jesus appears to be someone different than you thought—well, who are you then, right?

Most dark nights of the soul that I'm aware of (including mine) drag on for much longer than three days. Often they last for many years. But maybe, since Peter's was triggered by the very act that brought about his and everyone else's soul rescue, it was somehow super-charged—more effective more quickly as the crucible and gift of grace that it is. I'll bet other people besides him and Judas were having their own dark nights of the soul that weekend too.

In fact, I'd propose even Jesus had one. After all, right before he died, he cried out, "My God, my God, why have you forsaken me?" He was quoting Psalm 22. Many people have taught that God the Father really did turn away from Jesus at that moment, and maybe he did. But I believe it's possible that, just as God has been with people in their suffering before and since, regardless of whether they sense his presence or not, God the Father was there the whole time. Jesus felt abandoned by him because, carrying the weight of our sin as he was in that moment, he too, needed to be purified, or made perfect, as the author of Hebrews mysteriously says (Hebrews 2:10)—not from his own guilt, but from ours. I guess it's not surprising that if Jesus himself went through a dark night of the soul, Peter would have too. Remember—Peter was becoming like Jesus— even through the crucible of darkness and pain.

But now it's Sunday morning, and Mary Magdalene comes rushing into the house where, somehow or other, the disciples had reconvened. "Someone's taken the Lord's body out of the tomb!" She pants. "And we don't know where they've put him!" Peter and John take off running. We don't know for sure why. Were they outraged that someone might have desecrated the already tortured body of their friend and Lord? Or did they suddenly remember Jesus saying something about three days later being raised? If all the things Jesus had told them about his dying—which no one had wanted to understand before—had come true, could it possibly be that somehow that "being raised" part would too?

Whatever is going through his head at the time, Peter is catapulting himself toward Jesus again. This is his pattern. And this is the final reason I suspect Peter's fear in the courtyard of the high priest was more about the disappointment of his expectations of Jesus than fear of being killed. If he had denied Jesus only because he was afraid of being killed and then run away because he was ashamed of what that fear made him do, would he really have been in such a great hurry to see what happened to Jesus's body? He may have felt complicit in Jesus's death, and not wanted to look for the body. If Jesus did, in fact, turn out to be alive and Peter had denied him out of fear for his own life, it might be a little tough for Peter to imagine facing Jesus again.

But if the source of Peter's fear in the high priest's courtyard was the death of his expectations, then the instant he had even a hint that Jesus was alive again, he would have known that really, his previous expectations were too small, and that Jesus was even greater and more wonderful than he had imagined. If Peter wanted to be with Jesus all the time before, he wanted it even more now. Peter did have shame about his denial, as we're about to see. But he had learned at the beginning of everything that the correct response when aware of his own lack and sinfulness was to run toward Jesus, not away from him. The fact that Peter is acting on this default response of his shows us again that he already has a hint that Jesus is alive, and that all his fears three days before—that Jesus wasn't who he thought he was—were unfounded.

So, it's not too surprising that, even though John gets to the tomb first and is a little hesitant about going inside, when Peter catches up, he just barges right on in. Just as Mary Magdalene had said, the body is gone. But if this were the work of graverobbers, they would've taken the body *in* the cloths it was wrapped in, surely. And there were the cloths, just as if someone had folded them up and put on a new outfit. Peter and John don't know where Jesus is. But they know where he isn't. He's not in a grave. So, they go back to the other disciples. And Jesus appears to them all in that room that night and shows them that yes. He is really and truly alive.

The weird thing about Jesus after the resurrection, though, is that even though he was really—physically and in all other ways—alive, his resurrected body didn't work the same way it had before it was crucified. We know this because there are stories about him walking through closed doors. We also know this because sometimes the disciples, both men and women and even Peter himself, don't recognize him right away.

Eventually the remaining eleven disciples (with Judas out of the picture) cooperate with the instructions Jesus had sent them through his women disciples: to head back to Galilee and meet him there. That's another thing that's different about Jesus after the resurrection. He's not with them every waking minute anymore. When Jesus's followers get to Galilee, Jesus is still nowhere to be found. The disciples know he's alive because they've seen him themselves. But this awesome thing has happened—and now what? The only thing Peter knew before Jesus exploded his world was fishing. So, with no Jesus in sight and nothing better to do, he says, "I'm going fishing. Anyone else?" And suddenly we are back at the beginning of everything.

At the beginning, Jesus's miracles rocked—and changed—not only Peter's name, but his world. Now the close friendship forged between those two was itself rocked—first because Peter had thought Jesus wasn't all he had hoped, and now because Jesus has turned out to be even more. What is he supposed to do with that? What does that mean for their friendship? Can Peter still do miracles? Can he still cast out demons? What about the Kingdom of God? What does that even mean anymore now that the King has died and come back from the dead? Peter doesn't know and Jesus still isn't around to ask, so now Peter is back in the boat, with his nets, not a fisher of men, but a fisher of fish—and just like at the beginning, he can't catch anything.

He can't, that is, until a stranger on the shore calls out to throw the nets on the other side of the boat. Once more, the nets fill right up. Weirdly, it doesn't seem as if Peter makes the connection right away that it is Jesus on the shore, even after a second miraculous catch of fish. The last time Peter fished, there was a miraculous catch and Jesus gave him a new name and a new identity. It's about to happen again, but Peter has no idea. He needs John to tell him "It is the Lord" (John 21:7) before it clicks. At that point, the boat can't get to shore fast enough. He hurls himself into the water and sure enough! There's Jesus! Who reminds him with, I imagine, a touch of humor, "Go back there and help your buddies bring in that catch. I'll still be here."

Peter goes back and helps, and Jesus cooks up some of the fish for breakfast on this little fire he has going, and then Jesus has a chat with Peter. After the first catch of fish, when Jesus identified Peter the first time, the interaction was brief. Jesus gave him a name, a new job, and told Peter to follow him. But now they know each other better. They've both just been through a lot, and so has their friendship. So now, while Jesus is going to do basically the same thing with and for Peter that he did at the very first, he goes deeper—much like the boat—and involves Peter himself in the process.

In 2 Corinthians 3:18, the apostle Paul writes, "And we all, who with unveiled faces, contemplate the Lord's glory, are being transformed into his image with ever-increasing glory, which comes from the Lord, who is the Spirit." This is a topic for another book, but I have come to understand that the glory of a thing is its essence, and the Bible tells us that God's essence is love (1 John 4:8, 16). Paul is saying that as we spend time around Jesus—the human expression of the glorious essence of God—with nothing between us, we begin to absorb that glory. We begin to look like him, think like him, act like him. The glorious love of God becomes our essence too. Peter's transformation into ever-increasing glory has been going on since Jesus first called him "Rocky." Now Jesus is about to remove what's still between them and commission Peter into an identity that reflects even more clearly the loving image of Jesus himself.

It sounds like Jesus and Peter are still sitting around the fire with the other guys when Jesus begins his very personal work of redefining Peter. "Simon son of John," he says, "do you love me more than these?" (John 21:15).

Did you catch that? Jesus is calling Peter "Simon" again. He is hitting the reset button. He's bringing them all the way back. And Jesus is asking Peter—probably in front of the other disciples—if he really loves Jesus more than the others do.

This is a touchy question, especially in a group. In virtually every story of Peter, we've seen him launching himself at Jesus. Maybe he really did love Jesus more than the other disciples did. But I wonder if part of the reason Peter needed a dark night of the soul was because not only were his expectations of the Messiah getting in his way, but so was his estimation of himself. Maybe he really had, somewhere in the back of his mind or heart, an idea that he was the best disciple—that he loved Jesus best—even that Jesus loved him best. Jesus's question does not negate that Peter loves him—or that he loves Peter. But it does shine light on false assumptions.

If you're familiar with this passage, you may have heard some teaching about how the Greek word Jesus uses for *love* in his question (*agapao*) and the word that Peter uses for *love* (*phileo*) are different and significant. Increasingly scholars doubt there's much difference between the meaning of the two words, so maybe you couldn't do an official word-study on these terms. But we're looking at this passage—as we have all the others—from a storytelling perspective. Why did John record this conversation in just this way? He surely only heard part of it as it was happening. Because of the weight of meaning this story carries already, it's unlikely that John was just switching up the words to avoid repetition. At minimum, it appears that Peter hears Jesus asking him something that he can't respond to in quite the same way Jesus asks it—as if a couple were having a Relationship Definition Talk, and one person said, "I love you," and the other one said, "I like you."

From a storytelling perspective, it certainly looks like Jesus's first question calls Peter out on his own high estimation of his love for Jesus: "Simon, do you really love me with the highest, purest form of love—and more than these other guys do?"

Probably the rest of the disciples sitting there were fully aware of Peter's pride about this. When we're arrogant, we're often the last to see it, but it's quite obvious to everyone else. Jesus is gently but pointedly calling Peter out, in front of some of his brothers who were wronged by this pride. He's doing it because he is about to commission Peter specifically, to something special, but he needs to root out the pride and call forth the humility that will be needed for his special role. If we are proud in our assignment from God, we cannot effectively channel the glorious love of God to others, and they will be hindered from getting to know and reflect him too.

The dark night of the soul has done its work, because Peter is starting not only to get a clearer picture of who Jesus really is but of who he really is. "Yes, Lord," he says, because he does love Jesus a whole lot. But he also knows that his love is still very human and there's no way he could legitimately claim the highest, purest, divine form of love. "I love you with all my heart like a brother."

"Feed my lambs," says Jesus. The last time there was a catch of fish this big, Jesus gave Peter something to do that paralleled Peter's "secular" job: going from fisherman to fisher of men. Now Jesus is calling Peter—the man who is being transformed to look like Jesus—to a job that parallels Jesus's job, the Good Shepherd (John 10). All Jesus's people are Jesus's lambs—even Peter. But Jesus is also calling the newly humbled disciple to help him take care of the others. To feed them.

Then I imagine Jesus gets up. He motions to Peter. Peter gets up. The other guys start clearing up the breakfast and putting out the fire. "Simon, son of John," Jesus says, when they're a little distance away. "Do you love me?" Now it's just Jesus and Peter. Jesus is still using the divine, pure love word. And Peter still knows he's just not there yet. He can't even presume to be there. He's been becoming like Jesus, but the dark night of the soul has shown him that he still has so far to go. He again uses the term for brotherly love. "Yes, Lord," he says, "you know that I really love you."

"Take care of my sheep," Jesus says (John 21:16).

They walk a little further. Jesus asks one more time, "Simon son of John, do you love me?" Now Jesus finally uses the same word for love that Peter has been using. By choosing this word, Jesus meets Peter where and as he is and at the same time mirrors Peter's third denial. John tells us, "Peter was hurt because Jesus asked him the third time, 'Do you love me?'" (John 21:17).

Peter's not stupid. He hasn't forgotten his denials—or that Jesus had predicted them, and they had come true exactly as Jesus said they would. Peter knows what Jesus is getting at. He doesn't want to be reminded of that night—any part of it. He's hurt that Jesus brought it up. He therefore maybe doesn't notice that Jesus is being really gentle with him again, even while addressing this unspoken issue. Jesus is no longer asking about some lofty love that Peter hasn't attained yet, but instead asking about the love Peter already has.

It probably shouldn't come as a surprise to us that Jesus is a master at sweeping away the veils between us and him. Those three denials are unfinished business between Peter and Jesus. Jesus isn't holding them against Peter. He just got done dying on the cross to forgive it all. But Jesus knows that even though he has forgiven the denials, Peter himself hasn't dealt with them.

Jesus could have asked Peter twice if he loved him, given him his new job, and moved on to whatever he needed to address with the next disciple. Or he could have given Peter a lecture. Either way, those denials would have remained lodged in Peter's experience and memory just like his pride would have if Jesus hadn't lovingly addressed that. Both things would have affected his new role—feeding and caring for Jesus's sheep. Jesus doesn't ignore or lecture. He lets Peter sit with the sorrow and pain of the memory for a minute.

"Simon, do you really love me? Like a brother?"

After the pang, Peter confesses, "Lord, you know all things. (You know I can't manage *agape* right now. You know I disowned you three times. You know I didn't understand what you were doing. You know I thought I did. And also . . .) You *know* that I love you."

Then Jesus affirms his love for Peter by, a third time, repeating Peter's purpose and identity: "Feed my sheep. (I do know all those things, Peter. I love you too. Here's how you'll know it—and show it.)"

It's a beautiful moment, and if any of us were skilled enough to craft an interaction like this, no doubt we would have concluded it there, in the nice warm feeling of restorative love. But Jesus doesn't. In fact, what he says next almost sounds like some kind of post-forgiveness retribution. Something like, "I'm giving you this job to do, but because you kinda screwed up a couple of weeks ago, this is how it's gonna end."

What he says is, "Very truly I tell you, when you were younger you dressed yourself and went where you wanted; but when you are old you will stretch out your hands, and someone else will dress you and lead you where you do not want to go" (John 21:18).

My parents gave me a brand-new NIV study Bible for my ordination, and in the notes for this section, the commentator observes, "Remarkably, Peter served for three decades with this prediction hanging over him; he most likely died in Rome under the emperor Nero."[21] Can you imagine going through your life for thirty more years with that over your head? Let's say this story is just about Jesus calling out Peter's self-interest and fear and denials, and that the prediction is a punishment. Then those thirty years would have been a slog, and I'm skeptical that our final chapters in this book could then have played out as we will see them do.

But John gives us a last clue that that is not what this story is about. John tells us, "Jesus said this to indicate the kind of death by which Peter would *glorify God*." Even if Peter may not have heard it that way in the moment, Jesus's prediction is not a punishment. It's the conclusion of this conversation of love that Jesus and Peter have just been having. Peter is being transformed into the glory of Jesus the Messiah, Son of the living God.

His dark night of the soul was a huge leap forward in that transformation. So even though he does protest ("What about that other disciple?" by which he meant John, the one telling us the story), he doesn't leap up and shout, "Never, Lord! That will never happen to me!" Because he knows it did happen to Jesus. Peter now knows he really loves Jesus, and Jesus really loves him. It's not enough anymore just to be around Jesus all the time, though he still wants that too. Peter wants to be as much like Jesus as possible. At some point, like Jesus, he may be bound up and taken where he does not want to go. But for now, it's time to learn how to feed sheep.

FOLLOW MORE CLOSELY

Remember the walk you took at the beginning of this book? The one where you asked Jesus what your nickname is? Return to that walk location and find a place along it to sit down with Jesus for a while. (If there was a specific place where Jesus really answered your nickname question, sit there, if possible.) How do you feel today about being in this place with Jesus? Is there anything that is creating a barrier between you? What is it? Are you open to the idea of his clearing that "veil" away? Let him ask you if you love him. How do you respond?

CHAPTER 8

THANKS FOR THE GIFT!

Acts 2:1–24, 36–41

f the story of the Gospels were a fairy tale—or if the meaning of the gospel (good news) were simply that we get to go to heaven when we die if we believe in Jesus, instead of that he intends to transform our lives and do good-news things with us here and now first—there wouldn't be any more Bible after the resurrection, and we would all be living happily ever after already. But neither we nor Simon Peter—who Jesus just commissioned to be a shepherd of people more than a fisher of men—get let off the hook so easily. It would be nice if, after we have told Jesus we love him, or even after a time of "discipleship"—learning about and from Jesus—we could just automatically be like him. Or at least be enough like him perfectly and successfully to carry out whatever it is he commissioned us to do. But I guess, if Peter doesn't catch a break like that, we probably can't expect to either.

The last story we talked about is not Peter's last story. In fact, it is only after three years of apprenticeship to and identification with Jesus that we could say his story really begins. Peter has been rescued from a life restricted by his own self-identification and limitations, into a life that is more and more an expression of his true self, discovered in and empowered by Jesus the Messiah. While this rescue certainly will influence Peter's life after death, the Bible doesn't emphasize that aspect of salvation in the Gospels, or even particularly in Acts. Everything Jesus's first disciples are described as doing after the resurrection, including the hope that they preach, has at least as much bearing on this life as on the next one.

When Jesus reinstated and commissioned Peter to feed his sheep, Peter didn't realize Jesus was going to ascend to the Father soon after that. Neither could he have understood that, despite Jesus's departure, he was on the verge of becoming closer to Jesus than had been possible before. He would become more like his Lord than he had ever been on his best day. But he had no idea about any of this the day Jesus told him to feed his sheep.

Some days later, Jesus, Peter, and the other disciples all head down to Jerusalem. Jesus was killed and then resurrected there during the Passover season. Forty days after Passover, there's another Jewish festival, "Shavuot" or, in the Greek, "Pentecost." Passover is a type of new year festival. (Rosh Hashanah, the Day of Atonement, is another one, confusingly.) Shavuot, or Pentecost, is a spring harvest festival.

Jesus and his friends go to Jerusalem, therefore, to celebrate this festival, but before it even occurs, Jesus spends a few more moments teaching them all. He tells them to go into all the world and make disciples, baptizing them in the name of the Father and the Son and the Holy Spirit, and teaching them obedience to Jesus's law of love. He promises to be with them forever (Matthew 28:18–20). And then suddenly, forget forever—he isn't there at all. Luke describes Jesus as rising right up from the ground in front of the disciples and continuing on up into the sky until they can't see him anymore (Luke 24:51; Acts 1:9). Except, Luke says, right before that Jesus also tells his friends not to leave Jerusalem until the Holy Spirit "baptizes" them (Acts 1:4–7).

Jesus has talked about the Holy Spirit before. At the last supper, he even told the Twelve that he needed to go away so that the Holy Spirit could come to them. I'll hazard a guess none of them had a clue what any of that meant. Still, by this time, even though there remain some skeptics in the crowd (Matthew 28:17), they all know—and Peter for sure knows—that Jesus can be trusted, and that eventually whatever he says will not only happen but become clear. After Jesus ascends back to his Father and everybody is craning their necks upward to watch him until they can't see him anymore, two angels show up and assure everybody not to worry—Jesus will be back. And then there's nothing left for the disciples to do but head back into the city and wait to see what happens.

While they're waiting, the eleven, the women disciples (including Jesus's mom), Jesus's brothers (Acts 1:14)—who didn't used to believe in him (John 7:5), but came to be his disciples after the resurrection—stay together, praying, united, waiting, trusting in Jesus to fulfill his promise. And then he does.

> When the day of Pentecost came, they were all together in one place. Suddenly a sound like the blowing of a violent wind came from heaven and filled the whole house where they were sitting. They saw what seemed

to be tongues of fire that separated and came to rest on each of them. All of them were filled with the Holy Spirit and began to speak in other tongues as the Spirit enabled them. (Acts 2:1–4)

You know what this reminds me of? Three snippets from Exodus, where God also does some miraculous, fiery work, beginning to set apart a people for himself, through whom to express himself.

The first passage is from Exodus 3:1–5, where God introduces himself to Moses. Notice the parallels. Fire—burning on and in something, but instead of destroying it, enabling it to speak words of God:

Now Moses was tending the flock of Jethro his father-in-law, the priest of Midian, and he led the flock to the far side of the wilderness and came to Horeb, the mountain of God. There the angel of the LORD appeared to him in flames of fire from within a bush. Moses saw that though the bush was on fire it did not burn up. So Moses thought, "I will go over and see this strange sight—why the bush does not burn up." When the LORD saw that he had gone over to look, God called to him from within the bush, "Moses! Moses!" And Moses said, "Here I am." "Do not come any closer," God said. "Take off your sandals, for the place where you are standing is holy ground."

Before giving the people what we know as the Ten Commandments, God says to them through Moses,

Now if you obey me fully and keep my covenant, then out of all nations you will be my treasured possession. Although the whole earth is mine, you will be for me a kingdom of priests and a holy nation. (Exodus 19:5–6)

Later in the same chapter, God tells Moses to have the people take three days to get themselves ready to hear from him. And then, just before the Ten Commandments, Exodus says:

On the morning of the third day there was thunder and lightning, with a thick cloud over the mountain, and a very loud trumpet blast. Everyone in the camp trembled. Then Moses led the people out of the camp to meet with God, and they stood at the foot of the mountain. Mount Sinai was covered with smoke, because the LORD descended on it in fire. The smoke billowed up from it like smoke from a furnace, and the whole mountain trembled violently. As the sound of the trumpet grew louder and louder, Moses spoke and the voice of God answered him. The LORD descended to the top of Mount Sinai and called Moses to the top of the mountain. So Moses went up and the LORD said to him, "Go down and warn the people so they do not force their way through to see the LORD and many of them perish. Even the priests, who approach the LORD, must consecrate themselves, or the LORD will break out against them. (Exodus 19:16–22)

What do these Exodus story snippets have in common with the Acts passage we're looking at? Miraculous fire, for one thing. Also, God's surprising and overwhelming presence, amazement, and, significantly, words from the Lord. We've already mentioned that when he wrote his Gospel, John called Jesus the Word of God. Meanwhile the Holy Spirit is the Person of the Trinity who most closely communicates the Word of God, not only to people, but through people. The Holy Spirit expresses the character, the will, and the works of Jesus through Jesus's people. Or at least, that's what the Holy Spirit wants to do, and what the Spirit begins to do here.

Jesus is known as "Emmanuel, God with us." The Holy Spirit might be known as "God *in* us," but not in a way that indicates we generate God. Instead, the Holy Spirit is God in us by generating something of Jesus himself within our own human nature. The Holy Spirit brings the Word of God to light, interprets the Word in our minds and through our actions, and in this way brings glory to Jesus. The Holy Spirit inspired the writers of the Bible. The Spirit overshadowed Mary (Luke 1:35) so that Jesus (the living Word) was conceived in her without human assistance. And now the Spirit has landed on and filled up this group of disciples so that they are supernaturally able to speak words about Jesus the Word of God to people from all over the known world, in languages that they—the disciples—have never been taught.

Not surprisingly, the people outside the place where the disciples have been staying are drawn to this commotion, and they are amazed. For maybe multiple reasons. It's not, at first, an amazement at the content of the disciples' speech. "How are these yokels from up north able to speak our languages?" the out-of-country visitors to Jerusalem want to know. Of course, there are always skeptics: "Oh, that's no big deal. These guys are just drunk, that's all." This is one of these hollow excuses to explain away something that makes you uncomfortable, like the people who thought Jesus was a reincarnation of his own cousin. True, every single person on the scene right now is in Jerusalem for a festival, but it's the morning of the festival, not the time for getting drunk at it. Plus, I don't know if you've ever been around drunk people, but when people get drunk enough for it to affect their speech, it's harder to understand them. You may have noticed. They don't miraculously start speaking someone else's language. At least, not intelligibly.

So Peter steps up. He has changed. Of all the disciples, he's still the one taking the lead. It's not surprising he has become the spokesperson. But now he is beginning to live out the new job that Jesus gave him. He is about to begin his thirty-year career of feeding sheep. He understands that the Hebrew Scriptures have everything to do with Jesus, and he is able to explain them. Peter does this. Formerly a fisherman. Not a seminary student—but someone who has closely followed and known Jesus for himself.

Peter is not anxious anymore. He is not confused. He is not hurling himself around frantically trying to find and be wherever Jesus is. No—he is confident. He is assured. He is joyful—because he knows exactly where Jesus is. Peter knows that Jesus is right there with him and will be with him always to the very end of the age (Matthew 28:20). How does he know? For the simple reason that the third Person of the Trinity, the Holy Spirit, who is one with Jesus and the Father and who always points to Jesus, is living in Peter's very being—is speaking through Peter himself. Peter has everything he needs to do the job that Jesus has given him.

And so Peter preaches the first sermon we hear any of Jesus's followers preaching, and the first of many sermons in the book of Acts. He starts by addressing the skeptics. "Really guys," he says, "You think we're drunk? It's 9 a.m.—let's be real here. Isn't it more likely that one of our long-ago prophecies is being fulfilled right now?" And then he launches into a quotation of a prophecy in the book of Joel (Joel 2:28–32; Acts 2:16–21). When the prophecy was given, the people of God had just gone through a devastating plague of locusts. The people recovering from the plague had no idea this prophecy from Joel meant anything like what is happening in Jerusalem this Pentecost, but you know what the prophecy does sound like? That passage we just read from Exodus 19.

The truth is, everything in the Bible is connected. All the stories are episodes of one big story. The Holy Spirit is the one who helps us make the connections. Peter now has the Holy Spirit—or the Holy Spirit has him—and to him it is clear, it is obvious, that the prophecy from Joel is exactly about what is happening to him and to the men and women disciples right now. The Holy Spirit really is being poured out on all flesh—male and female, young and old, slave and free—and communicating in all the known languages of that part of the world.

Speaking of connections, get this: Originally, when God gave the festival of Shavuot to the Israelites, it was simply a spring harvest festival. But later in their history, the Jewish people began also celebrating it as the anniversary of God's giving them the Torah on Mount Sinai. The giving of the Torah was significant to them because it was in that act that God cut off their former identity as slaves in Egypt and gave them the identity as his special people through whom to bless the world. Nowadays, this festival is for the Jews a celebration of the birthday of the people of Israel—the people of God. Significantly, for Christians, this very same festival is a celebration of the birthday of the Church—the people of God.

We know it's not an accident that God picked Passover as the time when Jesus died and rose to deliver us from our sin-slavery, the way Moses delivered the Israelites from slavery in Egypt. There are lots of connections between the symbolism of Passover practice and what happened during Holy Week. So then why, when it comes to Pentecost, do Christians often talk about it as if the only reason the Holy Spirit came during that holiday was as a marketing stunt because there was going to be an international crowd in Jerusalem at the time?

What if, just as God built significance into Passover that would be fulfilled by Jesus, God also built significance into Pentecost that would be fulfilled by the Holy Spirit? It doesn't seem like a coincidence that God picked Pentecost—Shavuot—a festival which has come to signify to the Jewish people both harvest and the Word of God—to be the same day on which the Holy Spirit is poured out on all flesh—the Person of the Trinity who manifests and glorifies the Word of God, in part by bringing in a harvest of people for the Kingdom of God.

When God gave his people Torah, he did it because he loved them and was setting them apart as his unique "kingdom of priests and a holy nation." But as we read in Exodus, they couldn't get near God. They would have been incinerated if they had tried to have contact with God on the mountain. The bush didn't burn up, the mountain didn't burn up—but, given the insistent and solemn warnings from God himself, the people would have. And so when Peter starts quoting this passage from Joel, which also mentions darkness and fire and thick smoke, these Jewish and God-fearing people from all over the Roman empire may well also be thinking back to the Exodus story. They're being reminded of ominous stories of the separateness and unapproachableness of God. As if remembering that weren't bad enough, Peter starts telling them about Jesus and that it's their fault he was crucified.

Probably many of the people in the Pentecost crowd had heard of Jesus, but they may not all have encountered him in real life. So, Peter reminds them, "Jesus of Nazareth was a man accredited by God to you by miracles, wonders and signs, which God did among you through him, as you yourselves know. This man was handed over to you by God's deliberate plan and foreknowledge; and you, with the help of wicked men, put him to death by nailing him to the cross. But God raised him from the dead, freeing him from the agony of death, because it was impossible for death to keep its hold on him" (Acts 2:22–24). He eventually wraps up his talk by saying, "Therefore let all Israel be assured of this: God has made this Jesus, whom you crucified, both Lord and Messiah" (Acts 2:36).

Now the crowds are like the ones at the foot of the mountain before the Ten Commandments arrived, or like the ones the prophet Joel spoke to who were still reeling from the locust plague. They respond a little like Peter did, the very first time Jesus got into his boat. Peter had said, "Go away from me, Lord! I am a sinful man!" and the people, after hearing it's apparently their fault Jesus was crucified, and what's more, that he's alive again, are, as Luke says, "cut to the heart" (Acts 2:37).

"Oh no!" they cry. "What do we do now?" They know they can't approach God, and meanwhile here are all these people who recently had flames on their heads like the burning bush—

not burning up—and the skeptics are quiet, and the crowd is alarmed.

But Peter has everything he needs to feed these sheep, because he already knows the Good Shepherd personally, and now he also has God dwelling in his very being. Besides, he knows from experience that the solution to sinfulness is not to run away from Jesus—not to run away from God—but to turn and run toward him. So he says, "Turn around! Turn toward God and be baptized—all of you, like Joel said—into the name of Jesus the Messiah! Then your sins can be forgiven and you too, will receive the gift of the Holy Spirit. The promise [not the threat— the promise] is for everybody—you, and your kids, and nearby people, and faraway people—everybody who God is calling."

Peter is feeding Jesus's sheep. The food the sheep need is the Word of God—through the Scriptures and in the person of Jesus Christ. They need that word introduced to them and explained to them. They need to know that they can't fulfill the written word on their own, but they can "turn back" to the living Word who is Jesus and be baptized into his name. They can be filled with his Spirit just like Peter and the other disciples have been.

"Let God rescue you," Peter urges the crowd. It's God who does the rescuing. Not Peter, not any of the other disciples, and not the people themselves. But the people believe him, and they run toward Jesus, not away from him, by being baptized. And Luke tells us, "About three thousand were added to their number that day" (Acts 2:41).

That's more than three thousand people all suddenly full of God's own presence through his loving Spirit, when—before Jesus went back to the Father—there was only one, Jesus. There are greater things that will be accomplished than were done in the life of just one Jesus, as follower after follower after follower expresses Jesus's love and Jesus's life in their own lives, by the life-transforming work of the Holy Spirit.

We know the people who ran toward Jesus on that Shavuot morning were filled with his Spirit too, because the Holy Spirit is the one who enabled them to understand what Peter was telling them. Ephesians 1:13 tells us that the Holy Spirit is the "seal" of our salvation. The Spirit's presence in our lives is the proof that we're rescued from our sins and for the life of Christ in the world. It was also the proof that Peter had been rescued in just that way. Peter's identity has become so wrapped up in Jesus's through the Holy Spirit, that it is becoming more and more difficult to distinguish where Peter's identity ends and Jesus's begins, or the other way around. More difficult. But not impossible. Peter is not done growing into himself. There's more to discover. Jesus is full of surprises.

FOLLOW MORE CLOSELY

Peter has done a lot of running to Jesus, never more so than when he has a sense of his own sin or failure. In this chapter we saw him inviting a crowd of thousands to follow that approach. What is your first response when you become aware of sin or lack or failure in your own life? Do you run to Jesus, or away from him? Can you remember a time when you ran toward him? What was his response to you then? Is there anything between you and him right now? Ask him to help you run to him. What happens when you do?

If you want to embody this practice a little more fully and you are a runner or have other physical exercise that helps you, you could reflect on the above questions and then act them out in your body as you engage your physical exercise of choice.

CHAPTER 9

UNEXPECTED SHEEP

Acts 10

Back in the mists of time, when I was a teen entering young adulthood, a buzzword that divided people was, maybe ironically, *tolerance*. It's a peaceable sounding word, but people had very strong positive or negative reactions to it. One group of people touted tolerance as a way to bring peace: people's lifestyles and opinions may differ from yours, but you do you. Let them do them. Opponents of tolerance thought of it as a refusal to acknowledge that some things are just plain wrong and need to be dealt with.

I had a more nuanced reaction—probably directly correlating to my experience in high school. The word *tolerance* made me think of eye-rolling and sighing and "Well, that's just the way she is, I guess." Which didn't feel like a good thing to me at all. To this day, tolerance to me means "putting up with," and not putting in the work to get to know who—or how—a person really is. Back in the day, I felt tolerance meant not caring. It made me feel invisible, and I couldn't understand why it didn't strike everyone else the same way. Nowadays, I think a lot of people do feel that way, which is why more and more people are no longer seeking—or demanding—simple tolerance, but all-out approval or affirmation. It turns out, though, that God has something far better to offer us than either tolerance or affirmation.

God is fully invested in forming for himself a diverse people. But he values us far too much to leave us—any of us, even people who have been following Jesus since childhood, like, say, me—the way we were when he found us. When God has free rein to form his people, he confirms that growth through a surprising combination of usually very dissimilar people, who can only coexist through the presence of his Spirit, for the glory of Jesus Christ.

Pentecost is the template scenario of God's unlikely, people-forming work. By the time we pick up Peter's story in Acts 10, he and the other Spirit-filled Jesus followers have experienced persecution and even martyrdom. They have also begun to take the story of Jesus outside of Jerusalem and Judea. More people are coming to believe in and follow Jesus, being filled with Jesus's Spirit: Jews from the far reaches of the Roman Empire on Pentecost, then the sort of half- or hybrid-Jewish Samaritans. The apostle Philip even introduces an Ethiopian to Jesus and his good news. The gospel is spreading, as Jesus wanted: out of Jerusalem and into the rest of Judea and Samaria, and now to the ends of the earth. Except even the Ethiopian was a Gentile who converted to Judaism before following Jesus. So far, there are no Jesus followers who were not Jews first. Until today.

Until today, everybody who knew anything about it, knew that—unlike almost everyone else at that time—the Jews believed in one God and considered themselves to be God's chosen and set-apart people. They weren't wrong. There really is only one God, and he really did choose the Jewish people. God's entire purpose in choosing this people was to establish a beachhead to reintegrate the whole world—all peoples—into his Kingdom and under his loving rule, after our species had forfeited our place and authority there. The Hebrew people were chosen, as God explicitly said to Abraham (Genesis 12:1–3), to bless and ultimately enfold all nations.

But people are people, and we like to divide ourselves into little privileged groups. Many Jews at the time thought they were special by default, and then were kind of jerks about it, and many Gentiles thought Jews were annoying, self-centered, and irrelevant, with far too few gods. Even the 3,000–4,000 members of the brand-new Church seem to have had this latent idea that the way to belong to the Jewish Messiah was to convert to Judaism first. Which sort of makes sense. That was how joining the people of God had always been done before. But it is not what happens in the story we're about to look at. Which is why this story matters. Honestly, without it, probably most us would not be here. Reading this book, I mean. And trying to follow Jesus.

"At Caesarea," Luke tells us, "there was a man named Cornelius, a centurion in what was known as the Italian Regiment" (Acts 10:1). In one sentence, we discover that this new Cornelius character is not like anyone else we've met in the book of Acts so far. He's a Gentile for one thing, and he's kind of a big deal: he is an Italian officer, serving the Roman Empire, in charge of one hundred other soldiers. He lives in Caesarea. This is not Caesarea Philippi up in Galilee where Jesus lived and where Peter called him the Messiah, the Son of the living God, but Caesarea Maritima, a powerful city on the Mediterranean Sea. You would think that Cornelius has everything going for him—power, status, wealth, and the commendation of the most powerful empire in the Western world. Which is why the way he finds his way into the Bible is kind of remarkable: "He and all his family were devout and God-fearing; he gave generously to those in need and prayed to God regularly" (Acts 10:2).

Why is this remarkable? Because this God that Luke tells us Cornelius reveres and prays to is the God the Jews worship. The Romans were polytheists—they worshiped a lot of so-called gods and also their emperor. Cornelius is not a proselyte—a Gentile who converted to Judaism—like the Ethiopian in Acts 8. But he's been around Jews, and he has seen something about them and their practices and their view of God that is compelling to him. Apparently, what he sees is so compelling that his pretty sweet Roman commander gig serving the emperor-god just isn't enough. He gives away his money to the needy—generously. He prays to this "foreign" God—regularly. And it's not like he just added the Jewish God to the pile of gods he was already worshiping. No—Luke says he was *devout*. Devoted. Which means there weren't any other gods for Cornelius. Just the one. Even though he hadn't converted—he hadn't gone ahead and become a Jew—he had dedicated himself to this God, along with his whole family.

And then an angel shows up.

Luke takes great pains to make sure we know he is telling this story as accurately and truthfully as possible. This was important for both Jewish and Gentile believers in the first century as they tried to get their heads around what it meant to be the people of

God in light of Jesus, especially as relates to this story. It's also important for us, because it's the first proof of the underlying truth in this particular story: God may do the impossible, God may do the unexpected, God may mess with our preferences and presuppositions and make us uncomfortable, but God always confirms his Kingdom work through his diverse people, by the presence of the Holy Spirit, for the glory of Jesus.

Because this story is so groundbreaking and so radical (Gentiles can become members of God's family *without becoming Jews first?*), Luke—who, by the way, is a Gentile—is even more painstaking with details than he usually is, and he recounts every single important element in at least two different ways, starting with this vision that Cornelius has of the angel. First Luke narrates it himself. Then Cornelius's men tell the story later. Finally, Cornelius tells Peter about it in his own words.

What becomes clear in all this retelling is that Cornelius has a vision, not a dream. He sees this angel in broad daylight, while he is awake. Luke also emphasizes that this wasn't some hazy apparition, but clear: "He distinctly saw an angel of God, who came to him and said, 'Cornelius!'" (Acts 10:3). An angel showed up, approached Cornelius, and called his name.

The angel vision is important, but in spite of the three retellings, it's not the main point. God sends Cornelius an angel to get his attention, let him know that God is aware of all his generosity in God's name, let him know that God is listening to his prayers, and point him in the right direction. But here's the interesting thing, which begins to hint at the idea that God has something far better to offer than simply tolerance or even affirmation. The angel does not say, "You've been such a good boy, you are obviously one of God's people. Keep doing what you're doing, and we'll see you on the other side!" The angel could have said that I guess. It would have made everything—including this story—a lot more efficient. But this is not how we become part of (grafted into, the apostle Paul says later in Romans 11:17–24) the chosen people of God. This is not how we become the Body of Christ. We don't get in because we're "good." Or tolerated.

Also, it's a rare case that anyone gets into the Kingdom without any contact with people who are already in it. God is going to confirm the Kingdom work that he's beginning right now with Cornelius through God's people, with the presence of the Holy Spirit and for the glory of Jesus. The angel can't do any of that. The angel is simply a messenger. The angel's job is to say to Cornelius, "I'm not the one to usher you into the Kingdom of God. Your good works aren't going to either, but they've come to God's notice, and he has sent me to put you in touch with someone else who can show you how you can truly know God."

Who better for this landmark case of Gentiles being welcomed into the Kingdom of God than Peter, the guy who loved and followed Jesus with all his heart and was called by Jesus to be the first shepherd of Jesus's own flock? So, while Cornelius is acting in obedience to his vision, sending some of his most trusted men to find "Simon who is called Peter," Peter is going into a trance with a vision too, which repeats itself three times. In case, you know, Peter didn't get it the first time, which he doesn't. Also because if it had occurred just one time, Peter might've thought he was hallucinating with hunger or something. Also . . . we've already discussed a few other significant threefold interactions between Peter and Jesus. It's curious that a threefold food-vision is given to the guy Jesus invited three times to feed his sheep. It's also significant that the Jewish food laws were one of the most obvious barriers separating Jews from the rest of the world. God is breaking that barrier down in Peter's mind and heart, just in time to introduce a new flock of sheep to the fold.

Imagine what this must have been like for Peter. The food laws go all the way back to the time of Moses. This is a far more momentous paradigm shift than what often happens in our present-day Western churches, where people get hung up on "the way we've always done it." These food laws literally were the way the chosen people had always done it, ever since they became the chosen people in the wilderness. So how does Peter know this vision is really from God?

God confirms it. First of all, Peter has the Holy Spirit living in his life, and Peter spent so much time with Jesus in person, that he knows what Jesus "sounds" like. When the Holy Spirit communicates with him, Peter is hearing Jesus. Second, God gives Peter this vision three times. The repetition itself is confirmation, but it also matches both Peter's three denials and Jesus's threefold "Do you love Me? Feed my sheep" calling of Peter. God causes the circumstances immediately to match up with the message: Cornelius's men arrive at the house where Peter is a guest at the same time as the Holy Spirit tells Peter, "There are three guys looking for you—you need to go with them."

By now you may be wondering what exactly we're saying here. At some point in your life, you may have encountered the teaching that the Holy Spirit, having inspired Scripture, will not contradict it. But here we have God telling Peter three times— and then confirming in multiple ways—something that sounds like a contradiction of the very law that God gave Moses and the people of Israel in the wilderness. Does this mean the Holy Spirit really does sometimes contradict Scripture? Does it mean that God changes his mind? Or maybe that the Bible isn't as reliable as we thought? Maybe it means that tolerance and acceptance are exactly what God is offering as he urges Peter to diversify his Kingdom?

In fact, it's unnecessary to draw any of the above conclusions from this story. But we do have to read carefully. It's possible and even, at first glance, plausible to read this whole story as saying that since God has declared all things clean, anything goes. Except first of all, that's not what God says in the vision: he tells Peter not to call unclean *what God has declared clean.* Not what Peter has declared clean. And God still has something far better than tolerance or approval to offer—both to those already among the people of God and to those who are, at the moment, outside it.

Both—actually all—categories of people need to repent, receive God's merciful forgiveness, be baptized, and receive the Spirit. God wants that. He wants all of us in his Kingdom. He invites us as we are, but we need him to make us who we are meant to be. This is far more mind blowing than simple tolerance and acceptance. So, as God overturns Peter's expectations about who the people of God are, Peter trusts that he really is hearing from God, and invites these three Gentile travelers to stay overnight before setting out on their way back to their boss. When I read this, I think how funny it is that Peter invites guests to stay overnight at a place where he himself is a guest, but of course, Jesus once did the same thing, long ago, before Peter had even met him. The more remarkable thing is that this Jewish Jesus follower is already inviting some Gentiles to stay under this Jewish roof.

After that vision, Peter is open to the possibility that Jesus, the Jewish Messiah, the Son of the living God, is overturning his expectations again, just like he was always doing in person. So Peter goes with Cornelius's three messengers, and takes along a few friends of his own—other Jewish people who trust in Jesus as the Messiah.

It's worth noticing that both Cornelius and Peter bring in multiple trusted people to be present to their interaction. Both of them, in their different ways and from different perspectives, are aware that God is communicating something momentous and life-changing, and rather than hoarding it for themselves and making it a subjective and private experience, they each include a few people who will be able to witness and vouch for whatever happens next. In Peter's case, he is bringing along other men who have the Holy Spirit too, so that no matter what, when he goes back to rejoin the larger group of Christians, his report will not hang on his word alone. Then all of these Spirit-filled people will be able to evaluate the story together.

When Peter gets to Cornelius's house, things are a little awkward at first, starting with Cornelius falling down to worship Peter. Cornelius may have been devoted to the one true God, but he's still influenced by pagan ideas. Some angel told him this was the guy who was going to tell him about God, so he worships him. Peter's response—"Ack! Get up! I'm just a human like you"—is a pretty striking one. He is essentially putting himself on a par with this Gentile. But then he adds to the awkwardness himself: "You know that as a Jew I wouldn't normally hang out with you guys. But God showed me that I shouldn't call anyone unclean."

Rude. But of course, Cornelius and his household already know that a Jew wouldn't normally hang out with them. By stating the obvious, once again Peter—and Luke—are being very clear that this isn't Peter's idea. God is the one who has gotten this ball rolling. Then Peter shows some more wisdom. Instead of assuming he knows why he's there, imposing the story of his God-inspired vision, he asks for Cornelius's version of things.

And Cornelius makes it clear that God is the one who got this thing—whatever it is—started for him too. The obvious confirmation of God's work from both perspectives assures Peter that this really is the work of God, and so he tells the story that matters most of all. It's appropriate to notice near the end of our book, which we began by emphasizing the importance and power of story, that it is a story—*the* story—that changes minds and hearts, both at Pentecost and for Cornelius and his family. People's lives and hearts don't change solely on the basis of rules or cold facts. But a compelling story, especially about someone we know, can rewire our lives. The story of Jesus goes beyond ordinary personal connection stories, which are striking enough. His is the story of the Word that underlies all the truth in the world, and Jesus's story itself has power.

Peter is realizing, from all he's seen and heard in the last two or three days, that God wants people from all races and walks of life to be a part of God's family. God loves everyone, and this forgiveness that comes from the life, death, and resurrection of Jesus, the Jewish Messiah, the Son of the living God, is not just for the Jews, or even for Gentiles who have become Jews first. It's for all people, if they will accept it. Cornelius and his family— who have known all along there was something about this God of the Jews that they couldn't find anywhere else—don't even get a chance to say out loud that they believe the story. They simply believe it, and the Holy Spirit knows it, has been waiting for this moment, and shows up to inhabit them in just the same way the Spirit inhabited the three thousand people during that Shavuot celebration in Jerusalem after the resurrection.

Meanwhile, Peter and the circumcised Jewish Christians from Joppa—and probably also Cornelius and his friends and family—are flabbergasted. There is no difference between the Holy Spirit's acceptance of these uncircumcised Gentiles than of the original Jewish believers. There is no possible—or at least no truthful—way either Peter or Jesus's people from Joppa can ever say, "Well, I mean . . . the Holy Spirit was there, kinda, but not as powerfully as with us Jewish believers." If they could have honestly said that, this whole episode would be really unclear and would have given all kinds of excuses to the first century Jewish Christians to treat the new Gentile Christians as second-class Kingdom citizens. God doesn't give them that out. God treats these new Gentile believers just the same as the Jewish ones. They are equal members of his family, his chosen people. And so they are baptized right away, just like the other members of the family. God did it!

And God did it through his people. Specifically and mostly through Peter, the pebble who has shown himself more and more to be a chip off the old block. Jesus and Peter are still together after all. Somehow Jesus, the master craftsman, has taken the raw material that was Simon Peter and made him into a people-fishing shepherd. Through the Spirit, it turns out, God even unifies wildly divergent qualities within a single individual. The net is casting wider, and the flock is growing to include sheep from other folds. And still the master craftsman isn't done with Peter. He keeps building something more.

FOLLOW MORE CLOSELY

How comfortable are you with diversity? What is your experience of tolerance, intolerance, acceptance, and affirmation? Have you ever encountered a situation where diverse people were together in a way that did not erase their distinctions but where lives were still being transformed to look more like Jesus? Reflect on these questions a bit. Invite God's Spirit to show you how to participate in the full unified diversity of God's people. Then prayerfully do a little research. How can you get involved humbly and respectfully in your community with people who are different from you—whether the difference is race, ethnicity, age, economic or educational status, gender, or something else?

CHAPTER 10

WORK IN PROCESS

Acts 11:1–18; Galatians 2

uring my sophomore year in college, I joined the Gospel Choir on campus directed then, and still at this writing, by the inimitable Tanya Egler. Excluding a period in my early childhood, this was at that point the most racially diverse experience I had ever had. In my second year, I was voted into leadership in the choir. The position afforded me an opportunity to learn a lot about the experiences of racial minorities, especially Black people, in the United States. My eyes were opened to new realities, and my concern for racial equity and healing grew. But in a lot of ways, I still didn't really "get it." In my senior year, Tanya's husband Calvin challenged me to look toward a future in which I intentionally advocated for this healing, here, in this country. But my heart was set on overseas mission work. I moved to London and worked with refugees and other immigrants from around the globe. Racial and ethnic diversity was still vitally important to me. I just wasn't doing anything about it in my country of origin.

When I returned to the US in my thirties, my world shrank considerably. In spite of multiple efforts to the contrary, it is only recently that any of my contexts for life and ministry have included more than a smattering of non-white people. I continued to try to interact and even cultivate relationship with the few Black, Latin, Asian, and Indigenous people whose circles overlapped mine, but mostly I reverted to old patterns and assumptions. I wasn't actively racist. Just largely unconscious. Maybe something similar happened to Peter.

You would think that after the giant epiphany for the young Church—that Gentiles as well as Jews could be included freely among the people of God—the Church would have become an instant and passionate advocate for this groundbreaking inclusivity. The Jewish people didn't hold the market on exclusion. In the Roman Empire at the time there were mystery cults with secret rites only for the initiated. There were Roman citizens who received special immunities and non-citizens (even if they were born within the Empire) who didn't. It's human nature to divide into us/them.

But now the resurrected and ascended Jesus had communicated to and through his friend Peter that his people are different. Jesus lived and died and rose again to reconcile all people, not just one group, to God, and in that reconciliation, we would also be reconciled to each other. This was an entirely new kind of community from any the world had seen before. There were no special hoops you had to jump through to be part of this community. You just had to trust Jesus to let his Spirit inhabit you and begin to change your life. This is incredible, world-changing, good news—not just for the hereafter, but for the here and now.

Peter already had a big head-start at being transformed into the image of Jesus. Besides, now he has also been tasked by Jesus himself to be the human catalyst for this inclusive epiphany. So even if it took the Church as a whole a little while to get on board, you would at least think that Peter would have become an advocate like that. And he did. At first.[22]

Almost immediately after the episode with Cornelius, the existing members of the Judean church began pushing back against its validity. Luke tells us that the story of Cornelius and his family got transmitted correctly: "the Gentiles also had received the word of God" (Acts 11:1). That should have been enough. But it wasn't. As soon as Peter got back to Jerusalem, the Jesus followers there started criticizing his actions: "You went into the house of uncircumcised men and ate with them" (Acts 11:3). They couldn't contradict the fact that God had apparently done something, so they attacked Peter's own actions. They questioned whether the ends justified the means.

Which is, I guess, a typical human response, but the implications were somewhat horrifying, if you think about it. They're something along the lines of, "Well, if God wants the Gentiles, too, that's his business, but surely he can accomplish that himself. We don't need to compromise our purity and the laws he himself gave us by having to do anything with them directly. Peter, you should've stayed home." Or at Simon the Tanner's, which is where Peter was when the whole thing started.

Peter, however, is quite clear at this point that he was where Jesus wanted him to be and did exactly what Jesus wanted him to do, and part of that task was, in fact, to go to a Gentile's home and eat with him. So he tells the whole story, about the threefold vision with the sheet and Jesus's message to him, all over again, and Luke tells it to his readers all over again. He tells them what happened in Cornelius's home, including the fact that the Holy Spirit became manifest among Cornelius's family just as among the people in Jerusalem at Pentecost.

Then, just in case they still think he's being subjective, he backs up his argument with a quote from Jesus from when Jesus was around in person. Some of Peter's critics were evidently some of his buddies among the original Twelve, so they would be able to verify the quote. "Look guys," says Peter, "I definitely saw the Holy Spirit descend on this Gentile's family and friends the same way the Spirit came to us. And while that was happening, I remembered that time Jesus told us that John the Baptizer baptized with water but that Jesus was going to baptize with the Holy Spirit. Obviously this is what happened. If God is going to give the Gentiles the same gift as he gave us, who are any of us to get in the way of that?" Finally everyone is convinced that the whole episode was really God's idea. This Good News is even better than they thought. God is reconciling literally everybody to himself . . . and as people are reconciled to him, they are enabled to reconcile to each other.

Paradigm shifts can be tricky to hold onto, though. Especially when they challenge a privileged category. Even, apparently, when you've been instrumental in the shift.

Peter, having been tasked by Jesus to feed Jesus's sheep, mostly remained in Jerusalem to do just that, while other apostles and new followers of Jesus dispersed throughout the Roman Empire to introduce more people across all categories—women, men, young, old, Jew and Gentile—to Jesus and his new way of reconciliation with God and each other. One new apostle in particular, Paul of Tarsus, had a distinct assignment from Jesus to work with Gentiles. Peter's context, despite being the first person to welcome the first Gentiles into the family of God, remained mostly Jewish.

Years passed. The Church grew. But movements—even those catalyzed by the Spirit of God—grow through people. And just as Jesus-in-person invited imitation and transformation but didn't force or rush it, neither does the Spirit rush it. Along with genuine spiritual growth, some other things began to grow. Including some Jewish Christians' discomfort with having Gentiles in their community of faith on an equal footing to them. Gentiles were latecomers to all this. Jews had been given a whole covenant directly from God by which they had—more or less—been living for centuries. At least, all their men had a physical mark of being covenant people, regardless of what the rest of their lives looked like. The physical sign of the agreement between God and the Hebrew people was male circumcision.

The fact that Gentile men weren't circumcised grossed some of these Jewish believers out. Gentiles in general grossed them out. We might imagine that some of the Jewish-background Christians (the men who had had this operation done when they were only eight days old and couldn't possibly remember it) maybe secretly relished the idea of Gentiles having to pay with some pain in order to earn their inclusion into what they had assumed was an exclusive club of God's favorites. Jesus the Messiah was their Messiah, the fulfillment of their covenant. Surely anyone who was going to enter into the covenant with their God—even if God was surprisingly more open to people of different backgrounds than they once thought—should have to adhere to all the terms of the original God/human agreement.

Probably most of these people who have become known as the "Judaizers" didn't think of themselves as anti-Gentile. They were trying, they may have told us, to bring Gentiles more legitimately into the fold. Or something like that. In any event, their ideas began infiltrating some of the fledgling Gentile churches. We know the impulse to legalistic observance of Jewish law and circumcision was especially strong in the church in the region of Galatia, because Paul wrote a fairly short but quite scathing letter to them about it. These Gentile Jesus followers had begun following Jesus on the same terms as their Jewish spiritual siblings—the story and the power of Jesus's reconciling life, death, and resurrection. It was entirely by grace that they had been admitted. Why did they now think they had to earn their way in when they were already there?

Meanwhile, Peter remained in Jerusalem. There was nothing wrong with that. Someone needed to be there at the original hub of this young movement and what better person than the one who had followed Jesus so enthusiastically and been transformed by him so profoundly? The challenge, as Jesus's other followers multiplied and spread, was how to conform new ideas and other cultural understandings to Jesus's reconciling way. They had to draw on the Holy Spirit in their lives to discern what to do about things like Judaizers from Jerusalem trying to undermine the faith of new Gentile Jesus followers.

Paul was unequivocal that physically, baptism for both men and women was the new sign of this new covenant between God and people. He was adamant that grace through Jesus, and faith in that gracious Jesus, was the only credential to be included in this covenant. Paul could be adamant, because he had been working with Gentiles in the power of God's Spirit for a long time now. He knew what the pitfalls in their churches were, and those pitfalls weren't that they weren't keeping kosher or performing a specific operation on their men.

But Peter would not likely have had to wrestle through these things very much except in theory. Fourteen years into Paul's ministry, Paul heads to Jerusalem to meet with Peter and James, leaders of the church there, to discuss his specific call to introduce Jesus to Gentiles. Apparently Paul has already run into some trouble with the Judaizers, and he wants to make sure that he and the leaders of the Jerusalem church are on the same page, working with and not against the Holy Spirit here.

Peter and James hash through the issues with Paul and agree that Gentiles do not need to become Jews first to be full participants in the work and life of Jesus. They agree that Paul does have this special calling to Gentiles; they will continue to introduce Jesus to Jews; and they remind Paul not to forget to care for the poor as he travels and preaches. That, you would think, should have been that. The three most influential apostles in the brand new, expanding community of Jesus all agree that, in connection with Jesus, there is no status distinction between Jesus's followers based on their background.

The apostle's agreement is consistent with Peter's own experience with Jesus's Spirit and Cornelius, and it seems like it was consistent with Peter's ongoing practice, whenever he had occasion to interact with Gentiles in the middle of his work with Jews. Paul tells the Galatians that Peter "used to eat with the Gentiles" (Galatians 2:12). Jesus had made it clear to Peter not to "call anything impure that God has made clean" (Acts 10:15). Peter might have been able to say, "Some of my best friends are Gentiles."

But even though he had been at the center of a reconciling paradigm shift among the people of God, and even though he became comfortable eating with Gentiles, and even though he had agreed with Paul and James that the Gentile men did not need to be circumcised, it doesn't seem like Peter had to do the harder work of living out the implications when they were challenged. He might not have been afraid of Gentiles anymore. But he was afraid, apparently, of the Judaizers.

If Peter didn't take his own journey outside of Jerusalem, maybe no one—not even he—would have known he was afraid of them. But he takes a trip to Antioch. The churches in Antioch integrate both Jews and Gentiles—a mix of spiritual backgrounds coming together because of Jesus and operating as he intended. At least, they're doing so enough that Paul never writes them a letter. But he does write about Peter's trip there. It sounds like at first, all is well. Peter is there to check in on, and support the work of, the churches in Antioch. He joins them for meals. He eats with everybody. And then some Judaizers show up.

These Judaizers had evidently been spending some time with James in Jerusalem just prior to their visit to Antioch. They claim James sent them, but we know that Peter, James, Paul, and any other church leaders in Jerusalem at that time were on the same page about the status of Gentiles within Jesus's community. So it seems likely that either these guys didn't make their full intentions known to James, or they had in fact spent some time with him, but he never actually sent or endorsed them. Paul doesn't describe what they say or do when they get to Antioch, but whatever it is intimidates Peter.

Peter—the guy who had known Jesus personally, flung himself out of boats to get to Jesus, was one of the first to receive Jesus's Spirit into his spirit, took leadership of the very first church, and was commissioned by Jesus himself to feed his sheep—starts holding back from the Gentiles. He stops eating with them. He sticks with the Jewish background believers. Maybe someone got to him with a reminder that his ministry was to people of a Jewish background. But that was no justification. Peter knew better. He had experienced better. He had defended better. And now he was allowing himself to be backed into a corner and, by his actions, to undermine the transforming work Jesus had done, both in him and through him.

And Jesus is no longer there to help redirect him, to focus him away from the wind and the waves of other—possibly more educated—people's opinions and pressure. Or is he? Peter isn't the only person Jesus has been remaking all this time. Jesus's friendship with his disciples changed all of them in ways specific to them. Now that Jesus's Spirit lives among all his followers, this transformation is happening all over the place as people cooperate with the Spirit's work. Which is fortunate, because while no one is fully perfected in this life, if we succumb to an old pattern at some point, there may just be another in-process friend of Jesus's around, who is a little more like Jesus in the area we're struggling with, who can help us get closer. In this case, for Peter, the person is Paul.

Paul has his own short-comings, one of which may be a temper. But one way Jesus's Spirit has been working on Paul is in transforming him from one of the most legalistic, arrogant Jewish religious leaders out there—so zealous he wouldn't stop short of murdering Christians for their perceived flouting of the covenant between God and people—into a man passionately intent on introducing Jesus to non-Jewish people who had never begun to observe the covenant in the first place. This combination of personal history and a fiery temper are just what Jesus will use to get through to Peter right now.

Paul calls Peter out publicly for being a hypocrite. He does it because, as he tells the Galatians in his letter to them, "I saw that they [Peter and the Judaizers] were not acting in line with the truth of the gospel" (Galatians 2:14). Did you catch that? Paul is saying diverse unity is at the heart of the gospel. This unity is not an add-on or an option. It's a real-life picture of what the original covenant between God and the Hebrew people was always intended to do—supernaturally unite all peoples with God and therefore with each other.

That's why later in the same letter Paul tells the Galatians, "So in Christ Jesus you are all children of God through faith, for all of you who were baptized into Christ have clothed yourselves with Christ. There is neither Jew nor Gentile, neither slave nor free, nor is there male and female, for you are all one in Christ Jesus" (Galatians 3:26–28). He doesn't mean, as some might say, that these distinctions are irrelevant. In the context of his letter and his world, he is saying that these distinctions are irrelevant for *favor with God.* In connection with Jesus, every person, regardless of origin, occupation, or gender, has equal access to God and value in the community of Jesus. Nobody has to erase their heritage or identity to belong. Transformation—which is necessary for everybody, no matter their identity—comes from getting to know Jesus better in community with others who are getting to know Jesus better, as both Paul and Peter have found.

It doesn't come from trying on our own initiative to adhere to a set of cultural norms.

Which is why Peter eating with Gentiles, and then no longer eating with Gentiles, was such a big deal. He knew better. He even lived better. Paul writes, "I said to [Peter] in front of them all, 'You are a Jew, yet you live like a Gentile and not like a Jew. How is it, then, that you force Gentiles to follow Jewish customs?'" (Galatians 2:14).

Evidently even in Jerusalem, Peter had given up adhering strictly to the rules which Jesus himself had told him in a vision were no longer necessary. But Peter, leader of the Jerusalem church, had allowed himself to be intimidated. He had allowed his fear of people to influence his relationship with Jesus and the transformation Jesus and Jesus's good news had already accomplished in his life.

And he was too public a figure to be permitted to get away with it. It's why Paul had to call him out publicly too. Other, newer, friends of Jesus could not be permitted to think that God's welcome to all people was optional or insignificant or a matter of preference or even calling. It also wouldn't do for there to appear to be a difference of opinion among two of the most well-known Christian leaders of the time regarding such a core issue. Peter and Paul were public Christians, with public ministries, and their accountability needed to be public.

Paul doesn't ever tell us how Peter responded to his outburst. Peter does offer a friendly jab at Paul in one of his own letters later (he says some of Paul's content is hard to understand and— well, he isn't wrong [2 Peter 3:15–16]). But even the jab comes in the context of commending Paul's teaching to others. It's not like Peter had never experienced the correction of Jesus before. By this time, he knows what Jesus sounds like, even when the voice Jesus is using is another apostle's.

He also knows what it is like to rush headlong at Jesus and Jesus's way of seeing, and to do public, seemingly impetuous things as Paul is now doing. Peter would have caught the truth Paul was leveling at him, even if, at the time, it embarrassed him. So it's not at all surprising that, by the time we get to our last biblical record of Peter, near the very end of the Bible, we discover him embracing the wideness and fullness and unity of God's people wholeheartedly—enough to write to them—to us all—about it.

FOLLOW MORE CLOSELY

Peter seems to have momentarily lost sight of everything that the life, death, and resurrection of Jesus meant for transforming the world. According to Paul, Peter's refusal to eat with Gentile Jesus followers was a sin grave enough to overturn the whole gospel. Spend some time reflecting on or journaling about the gospel, or good news, of Jesus. How would you describe it? How have you experienced it? How do you express it? How does this episode between Peter and Paul adjust or challenge your perception of the good news or even your experience of Jesus?

CHAPTER 11

I GOT A ROCK . . .

1 Peter 2:1–10

n the classic 1966 television special, *It's the Great Pumpkin, Charlie Brown,* Charlie Brown and his pals assess their respective Halloween loot. Everyone's bags are full of delightful sweets, except our main character's, who famously—and glumly—says, "I got a rock." The rock is yet another indicator of Charlie Brown's haplessness and unpopularity, even though all the viewers know how loveable he is. No young trick-or-treater wants even to be given an apple, let alone a rock.

It's possible that, all the way back at the beginning of everything, when Jesus nicknamed Simon out of the blue with a name that means "rock," Simon felt a little like Charlie Brown in the special. On the other hand, in the Bible, rocks are generally no bad thing. The entire Bible makes it very clear that there is no place for idols—rivals to God—among God's people, and that people have a penchant for turning any old, created thing into a rival for God. On the other hand, the Bible also is consistently clear that the created world is good, and that sometimes it's helpful to have visible, tangible reminders of things that God has done. This, in fact, is probably why there's a Bible in the first place.

But also, stones are a particularly biblical sort of object to serve this purpose. I say that because there are numerous stories in the First Testament where God's people stack up stones for remembering. The most notable of these events is the one in Joshua 4, when God himself encourages the practice, so that the people can have a material reminder of the way God worked to free them from slavery and bring them into their promised land. A remembrance stone or other simple object symbolizes the story—and everything encountered and experienced in it— whether it was a story you were living or even one like Peter's which you've been reading and, in a way, witnessing for the last ten chapters.

We have spent the previous pages of this book traveling with Simon Peter on his journey to Jesus. Now we're looking back, wrapping up, and also looking forward. What has happened to Peter on this journey? What has happened to us? Where do we want to go from here? Peter was Jesus's first pick to lead and spiritually feed his people, and there is some sense in which everyone who gives their lives to following Jesus has something in common with Peter. Like Peter, we are following Jesus into what turns out to be Jesus's own story while in the process of being transformed into our true selves. Selves which, for all their increasing distinctness, look more and more like Jesus.

Remember how we started this book talking about stories? We said that stories, more than teaching, are what change us. We can tell the full effect of a story, though, by the way we communicate both in words and in action afterward. At the very end of the Bible, we find two short letters attributed to Peter. We can think about them as the lasting food with which he fed and still feeds Jesus's sheep. They are also the proof of a life transformed by Jesus.

Pretty much everything we've learned about Peter—and about Jesus through Peter's experience of him—has transformed Peter's way of thinking and spills over into his writing. We're about to see that everything he learned wasn't just for himself and his own transformation, or even only for the immediate sheep in the fold he was assigned to. The movements of Peter's transformation are for us and our transformation too. In his last recorded words, Peter will show us who, through God's grace, we are to each other and to the world because of the identity that's been forged by our craftsman Jesus, the Messiah, the Son of the Living God.

You may have noticed that in the first part of Peter's journey to and with Jesus, the life-changing interactions really zeroed in mostly on Peter and Jesus. Other people were usually around— James and John, other disciples, crowds, maybe some Pharisees and Sadducees. These other people—and especially how Jesus related to them—surely influenced Peter's own experience in some way. But they weren't particularly pivotal to what was happening to him, or what was happening between him and Jesus. After Jesus rose from the dead, on the other hand, he hit the reset button on his and Peter's relationship, commissioning Peter not simply to fish for people, but to feed sheep. A shepherd's relationship with sheep is much more long term, personal, and intentional than a fisherman's with the fish he catches. A shepherd and flock are part of the same community in a way that a fisherman and fish definitely are not.

Suddenly Peter's relationship with Jesus became both much more internal—interacting with Jesus by the Holy Spirit—and external—encountering Jesus in other Spirit-filled people. Transformation—and the whole connection with Jesus itself—no longer happens for Peter through the friendship of two guys on a three-year road trip, but in community with other people who are also getting to know Jesus.

Now Peter is writing a letter to start-up churches (let's be honest—all the churches at this time were start-up churches) scattered all over Asia Minor. One of the reasons these churches are scattered there is because by this time even "regular" Christians, not just the famous Twelve, or even the initial group of women disciples, have been introducing Jesus to everyone as they move around the Roman Empire. Also because of persecution. Since we don't know exactly when this letter was written, we don't know for sure what type of persecution these churches were facing when they received it. It sounds as if the situation is not as severe as things would get for Christians later, but severe enough that Peter thought it wise to write these churches to remind them of who they are in connection with Jesus Christ. He's writing to strengthen them as they face mockery and discrimination and worse, and reminding them that they are becoming like Jesus. Reminding them that Jesus suffered, so they—as they become like him—will too. It's part of the process. Peter, we have seen, knows that from experience.

Peter explains that who these churches—and the church today—need to be is a people united in Jesus's love. When the outside world is hostile, we need to respond to it with love like Jesus did, and we can't possibly do that if we're bickering with each other. "Rid yourselves of all malice and all deceit, hypocrisy, envy, and slander of every kind," says Peter (1 Peter 2:1). Where there are humans in this broken world, there of course is malice, deceit, hypocrisy, envy, and slander in some form or another. But "This is not how people being transformed by Jesus are supposed to look and act," Peter says. "You should be like an innocent baby who is totally focused on being nourished by his mother's milk. Don't be sidetracked by junk—only God's pure food will allow you to grow healthily into the salvation that you already have." There's that food idea again. Peter is feeding Jesus's sheep. Some of those sheep might be us.

Then Peter switches metaphors abruptly. After all, feeding sheep is not the only formative metaphor he has encountered in his life with Jesus. He's never forgotten—and now we won't either—that back when he met Jesus, Simon was a fisherman. And Jesus, a skilled craftsman working in wood or stone, gave him a new identity— "Peter," or, as we said, "Rocky." All this time, Peter has been growing into that new identity. He has let the skilled craftsman Jesus dig him up, quarry and shape him, and polish him. By this time in Peter's ministry, he knows something undeniably true: this new identity he was given is for all of Jesus's followers. For Peter, after all he's lived through, it is no longer "me and Jesus." His identity is only true and meaningful as the whole people of God share it—because it's Jesus's identity that we've all been given. As we keep digging into this meal Peter has prepared for us, we learn that we all "got a rock." Also that, in a way, each of us is one.

I really enjoy collecting pretty pebbles when I go to the beach or maybe to other countries with different geology than

I'm used to. But here in New England, for most people, including me when I'm trying to garden, a rock is not exciting. In this part of the world there are rocks everywhere. It turns out, though, that in Israel, the image of rocks and stones was kind of special. Not only did people pile them up to remember significant events and people, but the Hebrew prophets and poets used them as metaphors often. This is why so much of this section of Peter's letter is quotes from the First Testament. With the help of the Holy Spirit, Peter has discovered his own Jesus-given identity ("Rocky") in the Jewish Scripture, and, having discovered it, he goes on to apply that same identity to all followers of Jesus for all time.

In the First Testament, not only is God himself often referred to as a "Rock," but there are prophecies about a special rebuilding of the Temple. Restoration of the Temple meant, to the Jews, the restoration of their people. Their people, that is, being the ones God chose to imitate his compassionate authority, and in that way express God to the rest of the world. The Temple represented the place where God's realm and the human realm met—the place where God and humans met. The Temple represented the place where people were given their identity from God, from which to go out and bring God's loving order to the world.

When the original Temple was destroyed, the Jews went into exile, and even after a rebuild and an upgrade, they longed for the glory of the first one. Then in AD 70, the second Temple was destroyed. Since we don't know quite when Peter wrote his first letter, we can't be entirely sure whether this destruction has already happened and is in the background of what he says. If it has, the idea of the Temple would be even more energizing for his Jesus-loving readers, both Jew and Gentile.

Peter quotes two Temple prophecies, one from Isaiah 26 and one from Psalm 118. There's a "stone" God will set up to build his house, the Jews understood. People could line their lives up with it (with him), like builders line up all the other stones in the building with the cornerstone, or they can reject it (reject him), after which they will just trip right over him. We know that tripping over the Stone is something both Jews and Gentiles have been doing from that day to this.

But probably not too many devout Jews of Jesus's day thought they would ever reject the holy and precious cornerstone. Many would have understood these verses, and others like it, to mean that one day not only would a Messiah come and make Israel great again, but the Temple would be rebuilt—as splendid as the original Temple built by King Solomon. In quoting these verses, Peter is saying something provocative and radical—but also empowering—to the scattered and struggling Jesus followers in Asia Minor, and to us as well.

The "builders" (the people chosen by virtue of their natural birth, but not by virtue of rebirth in Jesus as the Messiah) rejected the chosen and precious cornerstone—who is, of course, Jesus— because they were expecting a different kind of Messiah. And also because they were expecting a different kind of Temple. They thought—as Peter himself once thought—the Messiah was going to be a military hero who would help them dominate again. Or finally. And they thought the Temple was going to be a literal building—a truly magnificent building, better than they had ever seen before. But still just a building.

Peter, in using these prophecies in this way in this chapter, says that not only did those people misjudge the nature of the Messiah, but they misjudged the nature of the Temple, because the new Temple, the true home of God, is God's united people. People who, as if stones were alive, have lined themselves up with the cornerstone—who is also a Person. This is how the chosen people become great—by approaching God through Jesus the Messiah. Heritage, as Peter soundly learned in the last two chapters, is no longer the determining factor. Jesus is.

After a lifetime of pursuing Jesus, Peter has realized, and is helping us to realize, that when Jesus took him from his nets and gave him his nickname, that was the key to the whole thing. This entire time—Peter's entire life—Jesus has been shaping him as a living stone, lining him up with Jesus himself, to be a piece of the Temple in which God will dwell forever. And it couldn't be—it could never be—just "Jesus and me." You cannot build a building with just two rocks. What Peter is trying to tell us is that we cannot be true, growing Jesus followers, long-term, without the Church.

Salvation through Jesus Christ occurs at first through an individual decision, and certainly we need to cultivate our relationship with Jesus on our own as Peter did. However, that only happens well to the degree that we are being built together with other recipients of grace like us—our spiritual siblings— together receiving the "pure spiritual milk" (1 Peter 2:2) of the Word and the Spirit.

In fact, individual as the first episodes of Peter's life appear, at least James and John—and often nine other guys—and some notable women—or even a whole big crowd—were around as well, as we noticed. They too, were being transformed by their personal interactions with Jesus. The individual stories at the time may have looked and even felt like exactly that—individual, independent stories. But in hindsight, we can see that part of how Jesus invited each individual into each one's identity was through their stories connecting with each other's in connection him.

William Willimon writes,

> Wayne Meeks, a historian . . . of early Christianity, notes that when the Romans looked at Christians, what they saw was a way of being religious that was peculiarly communal and therefore countercultural. Early Christians impressed pagan Romans as being essentially communal. Even those practices that are urged upon individuals in the privacy of their homes . . . are extensions of the community's practice— indeed they are means of reminding individuals even when alone that they are not merely devotees of the Christians' God, they are members of Christ's body, the people of God. This was how the Christian movement differed most visibly from the other [religions] . . . The Christians' practices were not confined to sacred occasions and sacred locations—shrines, sacrifices, processions—but were integral to the formation of communities with a distinct self-awareness.[23]

In other words, Christians were people who were letting Jesus define them through belonging to each other. They were identifying with the Body of Christ, allowing Jesus to transform them through their relationships with each other. And other people noticed.

As I write this, the Church in the northern segment of the Western hemisphere is going through a time of great upheaval. Ways in which the institution as a whole has failed to reflect what

Jesus is like, even to the point of committing abuse and injustice, are being brought to light. Truths about Jesus's way of love and reconciliation—truths Peter himself learned in the very first days and years of the Church's existence—seem, in much of the Church now, to have completely disappeared.

It is beyond challenging to continue to be a part of such an entity. It's nearly impossible most days to see how there is anything about the Church that was Jesus's idea, or that Jesus loves. Many of us have been so traumatized by things that have happened to us or others at the hands of the Church, regardless of denomination, that we have completely given up. "Jesus and me" is the best we can manage, and some have even given up on Jesus himself.

I have a feeling, though, that if Peter were here, he would pretty much write us this same letter that we already have in our Bibles. Because as he, the feeder of sheep, puts it, he himself has "tasted that the Lord is good" (1 Peter 2:3). And at least some of us have, even these days, too. Peter knows that our good Lord—Jesus, Messiah, Son of the Living God—spent his earthly life putting together the beginnings of an unlikely, diverse community, which he would infuse and empower with his Holy Spirit to be a representation of him still, in person, in the world.

As the forms of our communities of Jesus change (and in many cases they surely need to), we who are growing to know and love Jesus need to keep meeting together. Jesus intended it. He meant for us to encounter him through each other, as Peter discovered and is reminding the Church in his last recorded words. We must keep praying together and—with the Holy

Spirit's help—pushing forward to the point where we truly love each other, ridding ourselves of all malice and all deceit, hypocrisy, envy, and slander of every kind. We need each other if we're really going to follow Jesus—and if we're really going to be built into the House of God.

You, follower of Jesus, are a living stone, whom he is building into the Temple where God lives. *The* Temple—the one that fulfills the First Testament prophecies. God is much bigger than the individual human heart. Individually, we can only reflect God to the world to a limited extent if at all. But when we allow Jesus, our soul-craftsman, to build us into the House of which he himself is the cornerstone, we become the light of the world, the city on a hill, a Temple that rivals Solomon's by far. Because we are a chosen people, a royal priesthood, a holy nation, God's special possession . . .

None of those titles (people, priesthood, nation) describe an individual, do they? Also—haven't we heard them somewhere before? Do you remember how on Pentecost, we not only saw Peter drawing on Scriptural prophecies to explain the Good News of Jesus and the coming of the Holy Spirit, but we also compared the Pentecost/Shavuot experience to the story of the Israelites receiving the Law from God on Mt Sinai in Exodus 19? Peter may not have quoted Exodus 19 at Shavuot, but it sure seems like he has seen a connection, because he is quoting it here. When God gave the Hebrew people the Torah, God spoke to them through Moses: "Although the whole earth is mine, you will be for me a kingdom of priests and a holy nation" (Exodus 19:5–6). Peter even adds the term "chosen people," which is a very Jewish term, just to make clear what he is saying:

The people of Jesus—Jew and Gentile—are the chosen people of God.

And this is us. As the chosen people of God, we are a kingdom of priests. What do priests do? They communicate God to the rest of the world, and they mediate between the world and God—just like Jesus does for his people. What this letter of Peter's, and his whole life, and this entire book, boils down to is this: God is still setting aside a people for himself, to glorify him by blessing the whole world.

Peter knew, and is telling us, that this can only happen when we're in this together. We will "grow up in our salvation" (1 Peter 2:2) only as we grow together into this Temple Jesus is crafting. We are a chosen people, Peter tells us, "that you may declare the praises of him who called you out of darkness into His wonderful light" (1 Peter 2:9). We don't save the world ourselves, even all together as a community. But when Jesus the Savior is living by his Spirit through our lives together, those around us will meet him. As we love and serve him together, they will know that he loves them and is for them—because we love each other with his love that overflows to love them too. It happened for Peter, that chip off the old block. His life is proof that it can happen for us too.

FOLLOW MORE CLOSELY

Take one more walk outside. Try to choose a location that has a possibility of at least a few pebbles around. Select a pebble, a stone, a rock, and bring it home with you. When you get home, clean off the rock. Spend some time holding and examining it. What makes it distinct? Do any of the distinctives remind you of yourself? Keep the rock as your reminder of this journey we've been on with Peter and Jesus. If you are a part of a community centered around Jesus, when you see the rock, use it as a reminder to talk to him about that community, to ask for the Spirit's help for you all to remain united around him. If you are not, when you see the rock, ask yourself and Jesus what kind of community he wants you to belong to for now and where to find it.

EPILOGUE

t might seem strange, considering I began this book talking about how I came to realize God was not opposed to women becoming leaders among his people, and then came to be one of them, that I didn't really touch on the woman-pastor dynamic here. I didn't even touch on women's spirituality in any way, in fact—unless you count a few brief allusions to Jesus's women disciples. Instead, let's face it, I just wrote you a whole book about a man.

There are a few reasons for this, of course—some more obvious than others. You already know that my hope when I first began my exploration of the life of Simon Peter was to "prove" that the idea of stages of faith, or gradual transformation through connection with Jesus, can be discerned in the pages of the Bible, not just in the lives of the post-biblical saints. For better or for worse, as we've observed, the Bible generally gives us more information—or more stories—about men in the Bible than women.

As it happens, I have already imagined a Bible-woman's experience of transformation in the company of Jesus, through my novel, *Favored One*, about Miryam, Yeshua's mother. But I was in a different stage of my own faith and experience of Jesus when I wrote it. Also, because there are fewer stories specifically about Mary the mother of Jesus in the Bible itself, I had to insert her a little more imaginatively into the Gospel stories we have.

By the time I came to explore the dynamic of Jesus-inspired transformation again, Simon Peter and his greater quantity of already recorded stories seemed the person on whom to focus next.

But there's another reason I chose to explore Simon Peter when I did, and it is directly related to my becoming a pastor in 2019. The more I become my true self in company with Jesus, the more I believe representation matters, but also, the more I am able and free to see more points of connection with more types of people. I have fellow-feeling for Bible people I never even liked before. I understand them better, as—because of Jesus—I understand myself better. As for Peter, we may not share the same gender, and I'll probably never be the type to fling myself out of boats. But—even though I'm arguably not as fully transformed as he got—we do follow the same Jesus. We have both experienced what it's like to start out as one person and, because of getting closer to Jesus, become a better, truer, version of that person. Also, we're both pastors. Jesus invited each of us to feed his sheep.

Generally speaking, I preach sermon series, because, as you've discovered, I need lots of words and thoughts to develop a point. My third sermon series ever was entitled *Follower* and was about Simon Peter. That sermon series, plus two chapters, is the book you've just read. I preached "What's in a Name?"—about identifying Jesus and how that enables us better to identify ourselves—one morning and got ordained that afternoon. My dad preached the ordination sermon. It was on Jesus's commissioning Peter to feed his sheep.

Getting to know Peter as he followed Jesus has done more for me than just give me biblical ballast to prove a point about stages of faith. It has helped me read the Bible better. It has made me feel more connected to the rest of the Temple God is building out of me and other living stones—the whole Temple, past and present. It has also helped me find new ways to connect to Jesus.

I've loved Jesus for a long time. But I love him now even better than I did before I started this journey, I think. Watching him transform Peter has given me hope that he will keep transforming me so that I too—even I, a woman—can look like and express Jesus. Getting close to Jesus is bringing me to myself, just like it did Peter. I hope this book has helped you get closer too.

APPENDIX

I f you are still struggling with the idea Peter was so excited about by the end of his life—a growing, worldwide community of Jesus's followers uniting as a Temple for God to live in— you are not alone. But maybe you do wish you could have *some* kind of community with at least some of Jesus's followers who are in a similar situation so you could experience not being alone. Alternatively, you might be a person—even a pastor!— in one of those communities who just needs some extra respite or support to keep hanging in there with your people when times get rough. I founded The Pilgrimage during a period of my own disillusionment with the Church as a way to provide community-in-the-meantime for people still trying to hang on, or community-in-the-background to help people hang in.

I'd love to invite you to join us for any of the programs below if you would like to "follow closer" with Jesus and need a safe, non-church way to do that for a while.

SPIRITUAL DIRECTION

Spiritual Direction is a type of spiritual companionship where one person (Director) provides a time and place for another person (Directee) to interact with God "outside their head" in a safe, prayerful, and welcoming atmosphere for spiritual health and growth. During a session, you are invited to explore your relationship with God by considering questions including but not limited to: Where do you put your faith? How is that faith being stretched? What is God saying to you? How is God inviting you to grow more fully into the person God wants you to be?

STEPPING INTO THE STORY

SITS is a 12–week spiritual autobiography course, where you are invited to take a brave look back at your life in the company of a very small group of others doing the same thing, so you can take the next step forward more confidently. Once a week, participants meet for two hours via video call. During each session, we learn about how we can more fully enter God's story of the world with the help of some tried and true Christian spiritual practices: *lectio divina*, spiritual journaling, and life-mapping. In the process, we invite each other into our own life journeys, supporting and encouraging each other as we choose which parts of our own stories we will take with us on the rest of our journey and which bits we may now set down so we can move forward.

THE WALK

The Walk is an 8–week course on stages of faith, and you have already had an introduction to it through this book you're holding in your hands. The class is intended for both Christians in the church and Christians/skeptics/deconstructers trying to get or stay out of the church. In it, we compassionately explore the twists and turns of "walking with Jesus" as Christians in the past and present have experienced and expressed them. We'll also talk about Simon Peter's "stages" together.

In The Walk we explore where each of us might be in our journey with Jesus—to provide context and understanding for those of us who are troubled or concerned or confused either by changes in our own faith or by differences between the way we understand our faith and the way others who claim the same faith, express theirs.

If you would like to participate in any of the above, please visit the-pilgrimage.org for more information and for sign-up links, or email me directly at jenn@jenniferaglayte.com. Thanks for taking the time to read this book. I hope to see you on the road!

ACKNOWLEDGMENTS

his book was a community endeavor, and by that I really mean multiple communities helped make it possible. A community of communities, if you will. The first one I want to thank is the congregation at CBCSouthbridge, who ordained me and who let me tell them these stories in approximately this way for the first time. Close behind them are the eclectic bunch at the-pilgrimage.org, especially anyone who has ever taken The Walk Course and therefore wrestled out some of the concepts of this book with me in real time, notably the Let Down chapter.

Ruth Buchanan and the Storytellers Network provided me the coaching, the motivation, and the technical pointers to make those original sermons into the first draft of *Follower*. In between the writing and finding a publisher, a heroic assortment of early readers assembled. This crew not only read and offered constructive (but honestly, mostly glowing) feedback on the original drafts, but many of them also made themselves available to meet up with me over zoom—all together, even though they didn't all know each other—to offer encouragement and suggestions when I was feeling lost in the process. This is what true friendship looks like. Thanks Trey, Karen, Fayelle, Mitch, Amy, John, and Dave.

Then there are the somehow 102 other people, some of whom *I* don't even know, who believed in the book and/or me enough to financially sponsor what turned out to be a successful

Kickstarter campaign to fund the publication of this book. Amazing. Thanks to Tim Beals and Credo House Publishers for believing in this book enough to bring it to print too. I'm particularly grateful for the meticulous work of editor Vanessa Carroll, who made wise corrections, asked good questions, and encouraged me with her occasional "Love this!" and "Good point!" in the margins throughout the manuscript.

I dedicated this book to my dad (partly because I dedicated *Favored One* to my mom). But really, both of my parents have been two of the most inspirational people in my life for showing me what it means to follow a real, living Jesus from the very beginning. Thank you.

Finally, I want to thank Paul, my husband. I lived a long time before we met, but I know that following Jesus with you has made us both more like him. Your daily support of and partnership in whatever ministry I'm engaging in at any given time gives me the strength and encouragement—and quite often the perspective—I need to keep going. Also, I'm pretty sure "If It's You" would have been a different (and probably more boring) chapter if we hadn't had one of our Bible brainstorming sessions that day. Thanks, hon. I love you.

BIBLIOGRAPHY

Ávila, St. Teresa of. *Interior Castle*, E. Allison Peers, trans. and ed. Dover Thrift Editions, 2007.

Bauckham, Richard. *Gospel Women: Studies of the Named Women in the Gospels.* Wm. B. Eerdmans Publishing Co, 2002.

Benhamou, Albert. "The Numbers as Jewish Symbols," *Albert Tours Blog – A Licensed Tour Guide – Israel.* April-May 2024. https://www.albert-tours-israel.com/single-post/numbers-as-jewish-symbols#:~:text=The%20three%20previous%20numbers%20symbolize,guarantor%20of%20everything%20in%20Creation.

Biblical Archaeology Society Staff. "The House of Peter: The Home of Jesus in Capernaum?" *Biblical Archaeology.* October 12, 2021. https://www.biblicalarchaeology.org/daily/biblical-sites-places/biblical-archaeology-sites/the-house-of-peter-the-home-of-jesus-in-capernaum/.

Carson, D.A. "Luke" notes, in *NIV Zondervan Study Bible,* ed. D. A. Carson. Zondervan, 2015.

Collins, Jon and Tim Mackie. "Daniel and the Four Monsters," *Chaos Dragon* Episode 15. BibleProject, November 6, 2023. https://bibleproject.com/podcast/daniel-and-four-monsters/.

Earls, Aaron. "Was Jesus Really a Carpenter?" *Lifeway Research,* March 12, 2018. https://research.lifeway.com/2018/03/12/jesus-really-carpenter/.

Fowler, James W. *Stages of Faith: The Psychology of Human Development and the Quest for Meaning.* HarperOne, 1995.

Got Questions Ministries. "What is the significance of Mount Tabor in the Bible?" *Got Questions: Your Questions. Biblical Answers,* last updated September 21, 2023. https://www. gotquestions.org/mount-Tabor.html#:~:text=Queen%20 Helena%2C%20mother%20of%20Emperor,the%20top%20 of%20Mount%20Tabor.

Michael S. Heiser. "The Unseen Realm: Documentary." Vision Video, January 5, 2024. https://www.youtube.com/ watch?v=w9EW3ORjpU8.

Layte, Jennifer A. G. *Favored One.* Notes on Pilgrimage, 2019.

McClister, David. "Understanding the Transfiguration." *Truth Magazine* archives, April 18, 1996. https://www. truthmagazine.com/archives/volume40/GOT040109.html

St. John of the Cross. *Dark Night of the Soul* Third Revised Edition. trans. E. Allison Peers. Electronic Edition, 1994. https://en.wikisource.org/wiki/The_Dark_Night_of_the_ Soul_(Peers_translation)

Willimon, William H. *Pastor: The Theology and Practice of Ordained Ministry.* Abingdon Press, 2002. Kindle.

Wright, Nicholas Thomas. *Kingdom New Testament: A Contemporary Translation,* First ed. Zondervan, 2011.

Wright, Nicholas Thomas. *Mark for Everyone.* Society for Promoting Christian Knowledge, 2004.

ABOUT THE AUTHOR

Jennifer A. G. Layte was four years old when she first told her mother she wanted to write stories. Since then, she has found both more and less traditional ways to do that. She is the author of two published novels and is the founder of The Pilgrimage—a Jesus-centered online spiritual formation community created especially to tend to the stories of those who have been hurt by the church or are otherwise struggling in their faith and for pastors trying to care for them. Jennifer currently also pastors a small historic church in Central Massachusetts.

Jennifer's background in both literature and theology gives her imaginative ways of retelling the stories of the Bible and of others, encouraging people to live within their own stories better. She is an ordained pastor, a trained spiritual director, and an Advanced Practice Board Certified Chaplain. Jennifer and her husband, Paul, live in New England with two adorable rescue mutts.

ENDNOTES

1   St. Teresa of Ávila, *Interior Castle*, E. Allison Peers, trans. and ed. (Dover Thrift Editions, 2007).

2   James W. Fowler, *Stages of Faith: The Psychology of Human Development and the Quest for Meaning* (HarperOne, 1995).

3   Jennifer A. G. Layte, *Favored One* (Notes on Pilgrimage, 2019).

4   Biblical Archaeology Society Staff, "The House of Peter: The Home of Jesus in Capernaum?," *Biblical Archaeology*, October 12, 2021, https://www.biblicalarchaeology.org/daily/biblical-sites-places/biblical-archaeology-sites/the-house-of-peter-the-home-of-jesus-in-capernaum/.

5   Aaron Earls, "Was Jesus Really a Carpenter?" *Lifeway Research* (March 12, 2018), https://research.lifeway.com/2018/03/12/jesus-really-carpenter/.

6   Any emphasis in Scripture unless otherwise noted is mine.

7   Richard Bauckham, *Gospel Women: Studies of the Named Women in the Gospels* (Wm. B. Eerdmans Publishing Co., 2002), 113–116.

8   N.T. Wright, 1st ed. *Kingdom New Testament: A Contemporary Translation.* (Zondervan, 2011), Luke 10:1–24.

9   Nicholas Thomas Wright, *Mark for Everyone* (Society for Promoting Christian Knowledge, 2004), 113–116.

10 Jon Collins and Tim Mackie "Daniel and the Four Monsters," *Chaos Dragon* Episode 15 (BibleProject, November 6, 2023), https://bibleproject.com/podcast/daniel-and-four-monsters/.

11 Throughout this book, I'll use the term *First Testament* to refer to what is traditionally called the Old Testament.

12 Complementarianism is a belief constructed in the 1980s and held in some church streams that asserts that men and women are equal in essence before God, but that there are specific roles that each gender must fill, with lines that the other should not cross. I briefly describe my "version" of it in the Introduction to this book.

13 Got Questions Ministries. "What is the significance of Mount Tabor in the Bible?" *Got Questions: Your Questions. Biblical Answers* (last updated September 21, 2023). https://www.gotquestions.org/mount-Tabor.html#:~:text=Queen%20Helena%2C%20mother%20of%20Emperor,the%20top%20of%20Mount%20Tabor.

14 Got Questions Ministries. "What is the significance of Mount Tabor in the Bible?"

15 Michael S. Heiser. "The Unseen Realm: Documentary" (Vision Video, January 5, 2024), https://www.youtube.com/watch?v=w9EW3ORjpU8, 46:19.

16 Michael S. Heiser. "The Unseen Realm: Documentary," 45:51.

17 Michael S. Heiser. "The Unseen Realm: Documentary," 46:38–46:46.

18 Albert Benhamou, "The Numbers as Jewish Symbols," *Albert Tours Blog—A Licensed Tour Guide—Israel* (April-May 2024), https://www.albert-tours-israel.com/single-post/numbers-as-jewish-symbols.

19 Wendy Widder, email message to author, September 6, 2022.

20 David McClister. "Understanding the Transfiguration," *Truth Magazine* Vol.40, April 18, 1996, https://www.truthmagazine.com/archives/volume40/GOT040109.html.

21 D. A. Carson, "Luke" notes, in *NIV Zondervan Study Bible,* ed. D. A. Carson (Grand Rapids: Zondervan, 2015), 2198.

22 It's important to note that for most of church history, antisemitism has far and away been a greater and more present evil in the communities of Jesus than has Jewish prejudice against Gentiles. The Church fairly quickly became, and has remained, a Gentile institution, and with the decrease of Jewish followers of Jesus in the Christian movement, a destructive strain of anti-Jewish sentiment and behavior quickly grew up. The dawn of antisemitism in the church is early in Christian history and deplorable and deserves full treatment. Nevertheless, in this story involving Simon Peter, an opposite dynamic was threatening the young church, and the focus of this chapter is that there is no place in the community of Jesus's followers for prejudice and discrimination, regardless of who is discriminating and who is facing discrimination.

23 William H. Willimon, *Pastor: The Theology and Practice of Ordained Ministry,* (Abingdon Press, 2002), chap. 4, Kindle. 102.

www.ingramcontent.com/pod-product-compliance
Lightning Source LLC
Chambersburg PA
CBHW051424090426
42737CB00014B/2823